THE BICYCLE BOOK

WIT, WISDOM
&
WANDERINGS

THE BICYCLE BOOK

WIT, WISDOM
&
WANDERINGS

JIM JOYCE
Editor

SATYA HOUSE PUBLICATIONS
Hardwick, Massachusetts

Satya House Publications
P. O. Box 122
Hardwick, Massachusetts 01037
www.satyahouse.com

This book may be purchased for educational, business, or sales promotional use. For information write: Special Markets, Satya House Publications, Post Office Box 122, Hardwick, MA 01037-0122

First Edition

ISBN 978-0-9729191-5-9

Printed in the United States of America

Cover photo © Bene07 | Dreamstime.com

To my family . . .

my mother, Mary Ellen Joyce,
the family Poet Laureate, whose love of the written word is infectious,
and whose kindness is infinite.

my father, the late Bill Joyce,
a gentleman jock, whose work ethic, honesty, fairness, and love of sport set
the standard we all try to maintain.

my sister, the late Peggy Joyce,
whose spirit is part of everything I do, every day.

my brothers, Bill, Pete and John,
who ran beside me when I discarded my training wheels and still run beside me, steadfast and faithful, through thick and thin.

and finally, my lovely wife, Paulette,
my best friend, who tolerated all the time I spent on "Jim's Mistress,"
that is, this book and the website that spawned it.

THE START OF SOMETHING BIG

Acknowledgements

An idea, a website, and now the book. So many along the way deserve thanks. *The Bicycle Exchange* (www.Bikexchange.com), the online magazine that spawned this book, would never have gained notoriety if it hadn't been for the sharp wit and plain speaking prose of Andy Wallen, our popular "Ask the Mechanic" columnist. Andy sometimes gets a dozen or so fix-it questions per week and he rarely takes a break from the action, despite his busy bike shop and duties as husband and father. His unique Q & A section logs hundreds of visitors per day, and for good reason. A sampling of the 1,000+ Q & As found its way into this book.

Second only to Andy as the major catalyst for our website's strong traffic, and second to none in his careful editing and insistence on quality, is my brother Peter Joyce, who lent innumerable hours of assistance to the site in its infancy. Single-handedly, Pete learned the secrets of proper "meta tag" coding of web pages and he spread our name and address throughout the world of search engines and bicycling-related sites.

Two indispensable talents in the beginning were Jim McNickle, web designer, and Kate O'Kelley, graphic artist. Jim did most of our initial web design and was a crack troubleshooter during the first two years. Many of Kate's drawings still greet our Web visitors daily (one cartoon of hers is included in this book).

This book would not exist had it not been for the quality work of the contributing writers and artists. They are the real creators of this book and I cannot thank them enough. Mason St. Clair, editor and founder of the *Wire Donkey Bike Zine*, deserves special thanks for permission to use writings and cartoons from his delightful, content-packed print newsletter, which I highly recommend to all. A poem and cartoons by Mason himself appear in this book. For subscription information, e-mail masonbike@aol.com. Gianna Bellofatto, too, has been an especially prolific contributor and motivator since 1997. Likewise, Theresa Russell is a first class travel writer and I've been lucky to have her on board for many years. And though he is not included in this book, journalist Charles Pekow has in recent years done a super job of keeping readers abreast of national legislative issues related to biking in his quarterly "Washington Cycling Hub" reports.

We never would have been able to bring you Scott Roberts' excellent interview with Chris Carmichael if not for the help of Lance Armstrong's associate, Mark Higgins, of Capital Sports and Entertainment, who put us in touch with Grant Davis and Kerry Anderson, of Carmichael Training Systems. Kerry, Grant and

Chris were an absolute pleasure to work with, and all are shining examples of courtesy and accessibility, even when they are at the very pinnacle of their sport. It just proves again that nice guys (and gals) finish first.

I am also indebted to Tom Hylton, Pulitzer Prize winner, for contributing a fine editorial on the value of biking and walking for community and country. Cheryl Towers and Christine Cooper also deserve thanks for their preliminary work on the book. And I give a pat on the back to my cousins, Molly and Claire Hoover, for their important, last minute research assistance.

Most of all, I want to thank Julie Murkette of Satya House Publications for giving life to this collection of writings and cartoons, and for creating a book that can be held, cracked open, and read with ease. That's something you just can't do in cyberspace.

— Jim Joyce, Editor

CONTENTS

INTRODUCTION   17
Jim Joyce

BICYCLING AND WALKING   19
Thomas Hylton

KEEPING UP WITH LANCE   21
Scott Roberts

WIT

AN INVITATION TO THE OPEN ROAD
& THE LAWS OF CYCLING   27
Gianna Bellofatto

BIKE BONDING   29
Gianna Bellofatto

A BIKE-ILLOGIC WORLD IN PERFECT BALANCE   31
Gianna Bellofatto

ARE YOU A GEARHEAD?   33
Alan Ira Fleischmann

VACATION SURVIVAL FOR BIKE MANIACS
WHO TRAVEL WITH NON-BIKERS   35
Jay T. McCamic

SAFETY BIKE: THREE CENTURIES OF SERVICE   38
Mason St. Clair

OF DOGS AND CYCLISTS:
THE DIFFERENCE BETWEEN RIDERS   39
Jill Homer

WISDOM

A PERFECT BIKE WORLD   45
Gianna Bellofatto

JOY RIDE   47
Gianna Bellofatto

ROMANCING THE BIKE   49
Gianna Bellofatto

IT'S THE SPIN   51
Alan Ira Fleischmann

THE PRICE OF EVERYTHING
(AND THE VALUE OF BICYCLES)   53
Chip Haynes

IT'S ALL RIGHT TO RIDE UPRIGHT: AN ODE TO THE
MOUNTAIN BIKE AND THE RAILBED TRAIL   55
James Brink

BITS 'N BOLTS FROM "ASK THE MECHANIC"   58
Andy Wallen

WELL HELLO THERE, ED! (LONG SEE, NO TIME)   67
Chip Haynes

SNAP, RATTLE, CRUNCH, BANG!   69
Chip Haynes

IS BICYCLING ALL THAT BAD? YOU'D RATHER DO THIS?   71
Chip Haynes

THE NEXT 30 YEARS? (HOW ABOUT THE NEXT 50?)   73
Chip Haynes

SHIFTING AHEAD: PREDICTIONS FOR CYCLING
IN THE 21ST CENTURY   75
Richard Fries, Maurice Tierney and Jim Joyce

WANDERINGS

REMEMBERING HANK   81
Jim Joyce

VERMONT'S FINEST   86
Jim Joyce

CALIFORNIA ANGEL   90
Bill Joyce

DESERT STORM   92
John Stuart Clark

SAHARAN MARGINS   97
John Stuart Clark

THE ANTHROPOLOGY OF FANATICISM: A MULTICULTURAL
STUDY OF WHEEL-LOVERS AT AMSTEL GOLD   104
Ella Lawrence

MAGIC (RE)VISITED AT WOODSTOCK   107
Alan Ira Fleischmann

OUR BEST DAY EVER   111
Geoffrey Husband

SPINNING HIS WAY INTO HISTORY   114
Jim Joyce

BEYOND THE STREETCAR. WAY BEYOND.   117
Ted Katauskas

GREASY FOOD, DRESS SOCKS AND THE MOUNTAINS   119
Bradley Swink

RIDING BUDDIES   122
Cathy Dion

CROSS COUNTRY TANDEM TRIP: A JOURNAL   125
Rhona & Dave Fritsch

BICYCLE TOURING IN YOUR OWN BACKYARD   141
Theresa Russell

CONTRIBUTORS   143

CYCLOTOON

BY NEAL SKORPEN

nskorpen@earthlink.net

www.nealskorpen.com

INTRODUCTION

This book is a celebration of the bicycle by people who ride. It's a tribute to one of the finest, most efficient, most useful machines ever invented.

Bicyclists are good people and they are everywhere. They are in every nation, every continent, every hemisphere, and even in the Blogosphere! They bike the alleys of downtowns, the cobblestones of old neighborhoods, the cul-de-sacs of new housing plans, the dusty roads of farms, the backwoods trails of state parks, and the asphalt and gravel paths that once carried the great railroads. They come from the city, the country, the small town, the suburbs, the exurbs, the college campus. They are all ages. They belong to every race, ethnic group and religion. Their sheer numbers rank second only to walkers (and many do both regularly) in studies about exercise habits.

They ride for every reason imaginable – commuting to work or school, fitness, relaxation, rehabilitation, family time, package delivery, law enforcement, romance, performing stunts, the thrill of competition, personal satisfaction, and in rare cases, for the glory and fortune of being the very best in the world.

Biking immensely benefits society. Whether it's lowering health care costs, trimming obesity, warding off diabetes (and other diseases on the rise), reducing pollution, conserving oil, easing traffic congestion, connecting communities, or keeping sprawl in check – bicycling is part of the solution. Besides, it's good, clean fun with no downside.

In celebration, and in the spirit of our website, *The Bicycle Exchange* (www. Bikexchange.com), I've compiled articles, essays, cartoons, and even a poem that represent a wide range of cyclists and experiences on two wheels. Six articles and twenty cartoons herein have never appeared on our website. The works are delineated into the sections of Wit, Wisdom and – naturally, the biggest – Wanderings. The contributors are talented writers and cartoonists, each with a unique take on bicycling. Whether it's in critical observation, in concern, in memorial, in fact, or in jest, each story and cartoon is definitely worth a look. You don't have to be a cycling expert to read this book; there's something here for everyone.

Thomas Hylton, a Pulitzer Prize-winning author and newspaper columnist, kicks off the collection with "Bicycling and Walking," a sensible, prescriptive editorial on why cycling-friendly communities are winners. On his heels is "Keeping Up With Lance," Scott Roberts' exclusive, one-on-one interview with Chris Carmichael, Lance Armstrong's long time coach and dear friend. Scott gets to the heart of the matter with Chris, and the matter is all about heart and discipline. Later on, two prominent names in cycling journalism – Richard Fries of *The Ride* and *Bike Culture*, and Maurice Tierney of *Dirt Rag* – comment on the future of bicycling. From "across the pond," Scotsman John Stuart Clark, a.k.a. Brick, contributes two exhilarating accounts from two deserts on two continents. Bill Joyce, a national Catholic Press Association Award winner, recalls an encounter on New Years Day, after double flats left him stranded. Though I give him more grief than he deserves (hey, he's my oldest brother), I am very proud to have his contribution.

Gianna Bellofatto's *Life Is a Bike* series is ever clever, pleasantly quirky, and always an American original. Alan Ira Fleischmann's pieces celebrate the "geek" aspect in all cyclists; he also lends a story that will jog some baby boomers' fuzzy memories. Chip Haynes' curmudgeonly style makes me smile and shake my head (and reminds me a bit of Andy Rooney, a personal favorite). Also included is a no-baloney sampling of Q & As from our online "Ask the Mechanic" column, featuring Andy Wallen, bike shop owner, who has fielded fix-it questions from cyberspace since 1996.

Other contributors include: Newspaper editor and touring cyclist, Jill Homer; travel writer and bike book author, Theresa Russell; magazine editor and daily bike commuter, Ted Katauskas; writer, editor, and former racer, Brad Swink; owner of Breton (France) Bikes Cycling Holidays and former editor of *Cyber Cyclist*, Geoff Husband; *Wire Donkey Bike Zine* editor and founder, Mason St. Clair; faithful rider and frequent *Wire Donkey* contributor, Cathy Dion; lawyer Jay McCamic, a certified bike maniac (by his own admission); fellow attorney Jim Brink; promising young writer, Ella Lawrence; and the cross-country tandem riding, husband-wife duo, Dave and Rhona Fritsch.

The most entertaining pages of this book, however, just may be the cartoons. Sometimes zany, sometimes topical, sometimes sobering – but most times hilarious – they represent the best works of a group of talented cartoonists, including Jonny Hawkins, Neal Skorpen, Bob Lafay, Andy Singer, Bob LaDrew, Kate O'Kelley, John Stuart Clark, and Mason St. Clair, the only individual to contribute both a poem and cartoon.

So hang up the cleats and the helmet. Take off the cycling gloves. Remove the shades for a spell. You won't need tools or a patch kit. And, for goodness sake, forget about that cycling computer.

This tour starts now. So glad you came along for the ride.

Jim Joyce
Emsworth (Pittsburgh), Pennsylvania
October 2007

PROLOGUE

BICYCLING AND WALKING

By Thomas Hylton

*Mr. Hylton is a Pulitzer Prize-winning newspaper columnist
and author of* Save Our Land, Save Our Towns.

Although mass transportation consumes far less energy and space than cars, there are even better ways to get around for short trips: bicycling and walking.

One quarter of all trips in America cover less than a mile. Most people can walk a mile in fifteen minutes, and on a bicycle, such a trip takes no more than five to eight minutes. Walking and bicycling instead of driving saves people money and reduces the need for expansive (and expensive) highways and parking lots.

Walking and bicycling as part of daily life can also solve the growing obesity problem. More than half of all Americans are overweight – double the percentage of just thirty years ago – and obesity is now second only to smoking as the leading

DO YOU THINK THEY'RE TRYING TO TELL US SOMETHING, ALF?

cause of premature death. The Centers for Disease Control recommends Americans should exercise at least a half hour daily to prevent diabetes, heart disease, and a raft of other illnesses, but most Americans don't exercise at all.

John Pucher, a Rutgers University expert on transportation systems, reports that in the metropolitan areas of western Europe, anywhere from sixteen to forty-six percent of all trips are made by walking or riding a bicycle. That's an enormous amount of energy saved, air pollution prevented, and traffic congestion eliminated.

The Dutch, especially, have implemented a wide range of policies during the last two decades to simultaneously encourage walking and bicycling while dramatically lowering bicycle and pedestrian fatality rates.

"In the 1970s we were building more highways to ease congestion," says Dutch planner Harry van Veneendaal, "but as the highways just filled up with cars, we realized they were only a temporary solution and not sustainable. So we stopped the policy of just giving in to motorists."

In the Netherlands, dedicated bicycle lanes adjoin virtually every street and many lead places cars cannot go. Cycling is routine for folks for all ages: children, young people (even on dates!), men in business suits, carefully coiffed women, the elderly.

In fact, half of all trips are made by walking or riding a bicycle. This means Dutch cities and towns are not checkerboarded with surface parking lots. It means they are quiet. It means the streets are alive with people, integrating the old and young to a degree seldom seen in this country. The Dutch maintain a strict separation between towns and countryside, and compact development allows everyone to enjoy the great outdoors.

In Amsterdam, you can safely ride a bicycle from the heart of the downtown to open countryside in twenty-five minutes. Residents of smaller cities and towns are five to ten minutes from green pastures. Thanks to separated bike lanes and the occasional motorized cart, even the elderly can get to the beach without assistance, or amble through the countryside.

"There's no reason we can't build dedicated bicycle lanes and take other measures to integrate walking and bicycling into the daily routines of Americans," Pucher says. "That would be the least expensive and most reliable way to ensure adequate levels of daily exercise."

🚲 🚲 🚲

KEEPING UP WITH LANCE
AN INTERVIEW WITH LANCE ARMSTRONG'S COACH AND GREAT FRIEND, CHRIS CARMICHAEL

By Scott Roberts

Chris Carmichael and Lance Armstrong have been through both the most difficult and the most glorious of times, and all points in between. Chris was Lance's coach when he started his rise to stardom and they have stuck together ever since. Chris has authored several books, is a columnist, and is the head of Carmichael Training Systems (*www. trainright.com*), *a business that coordinates training programs for all types of athletes – from the world class, elite cyclist, to the amateur eyeing that first triathlon. Scott Roberts, of Oil City, Pennsylvania, is an avid cyclist and veteran sports reporter.*

Scott Roberts: I'll assume that while you were training Lance Armstrong he was your top priority as far as clients go. How has your life changed since he retired from cycling?

Chris Carmichael: You know, I get this question pretty frequently, and I think the following answer I wrote for an earlier interview sums it up pretty well:

> I have a lot more time to spend with my family and more time to focus on building Carmichael Training Systems. I've also spent more hours on my bike and I'm in better shape than I've been in for years. One of my biggest projects since Lance retired has been writing my new book, 5 *Essentials for a Winning Life*. When I took a step back and looked at my life, at Lance's, and at the lives of the thousands of athletes coached by CTS, I realized that the people who achieved the greatest success were those who committed to supporting their health, career, fitness, nutrition, and relationships simultaneously. My life was out of balance for a long time, and I made important changes to regain a high-performance life. I'm accomplishing more, sustaining better relationships with my wife and children; my weight is down and my blood pressure is lower; I'm sleeping better, feeling less stressed, and I have more energy. When I realized that the concepts that were working for me and thousands of CTS members applied just as well to non-athletes, I immediately set to work writing the book so I can get that message out to as many people as possible.

SR: When Armstrong was contemplating coming out of retirement and going for an eighth Tour de France win did he seek your advice, and if so, what did you say?

CC: I don't think people really realize how ready Lance was to retire, and no amount of goading is going to get him back into the professional peloton. Knowing when to step away is hard for some athletes, but it was a clear choice for Lance. He chose to go out on top, to retire from the top step of the podium on the Champs Elysees, on his terms, like a champion. Retiring has given him the opportunity to spend more time on other immensely valuable areas of his life, namely his children and his foundation.

SR: As a trainer, how much has the BALCO scandal put a black mark on your profession? (Note: BALCO is short for the now infamous Bay Area Laboratory Cooperative, the organization that allegedly provided many famous athletes – Barry Bonds included – performance enhancing drugs designed to evade detection by drug testing.)

CC: The way I see it, the drug scandals just make me even more committed to educating a new breed of coaches and providing a work environment where they can develop their skills and thrive without the pressure of resorting to performance enhancing drugs. I can't control what unscrupulous coaches or athletes choose to do, but I can use the resources available to me to make sure that Carmichael Training Systems is the place where clean athletes can work with honest coaches.

SR: Do you think there is anything Lance Armstrong can do to silence the accusers of him not racing clean?

CC: I think he's doing it, slowly, by contesting the allegations and confronting his accusers. When they're pressed to back up their allegations with proof, the facts have always supported Lance. When you have the truth on your side, there's no reason to back away from a challenge.

SR: When he was accused, as his trainer, how much did this insult you as well?

CC: I've developed a pretty thick skin over the years. I know the truth, so I go to sleep with a clear conscience every night.

SR: With the BALCO scandal, steroids in baseball and track, and the 2006 Tour winner testing positive, has cycling fallen into that pit of doubt where anyone who wins or does well is assumed to be a cheater?

CC: I certainly hope not. There are athletes at the top of every sport who have achieved their dreams with hard work, determination, and great skill – not drugs. At the same time, there's no doubt that performance-enhancing drugs have affected competitions from high school through the highest reaches of professional sports. For the situation to get better clean athletes have to persevere and we all have to support honest, transparent testing procedures that equally protect the innocent and punish the guilty.

SR: How are trainers who are caught helping their clients cheat thought of by those who work to train their clients legitimately?

CC: I can't speak for anyone else, but I don't spend a lot of time thinking about coaches who help athletes cheat. I support in- and out-of-competition drug testing and the organizations that exist to catch cheaters. I'll leave the job of rooting out dishonest athletes and coaches to the anti-doping officials; I spend my time working with clean athletes and educating coaches so they can develop clean champions.

SR: Do you ever see a day where doping in cycling is considered a crime that is punishable by law?

CC: I'd rather spend more law enforcement resources to eradicate violent crimes against women and children first. In other words, doping in cycling is a serious problem, but one that the sport and anti-doping organizations can work together to fix. Law enforcement has bigger problems to tackle.

SR: Does Lance still seek your help to stay in shape or has he really retired and become a couch potato like the rest of America?

CC: Lance and I still talk frequently, but these days we talk about our kids about as much as we talk about training. The New York City Marathon was a big challenge for Lance, and we almost raced together in the Leadville 100 mountain bike race in Colorado. He may not be a professional cyclist anymore, but the athlete inside of him didn't disappear when he retired. And Lance's biggest challenge right now is the same one thousands of busy adults face: time management. He has a hectic travel schedule and a lot of demands on his time, so when we talk about training it often has to do with getting the most out of limited exercise time.

SR: Do you believe that Americans need to have a Tour de France champion to stay interested in the sport of Cycling?

CC: Twenty years ago, yes. The world's a much smaller place now, though. In the 1980s, Tour de France coverage was in the September issue of American cycling magazines. Now you can get live coverage on television and a dozen websites. Sports are becoming less provincial and more global, and more extensive coverage of cycling helps keep fans engaged throughout the year. Of course, an American winning the Tour de France certainly doesn't hurt.

♾ ♾ ♾

WIT

Wit has truth in it: wisecracking is simply calisthenics with words.
— Dorothy Parker

An Invitation to the Open Road & the Laws of Cycling
Life is a Bike©

By Gianna Bellofatto

This is the first of Gianna's unforgettable Life is a Bike *essays.*
Step aside Newton and Murphy. . . .

The time is now. This is an invitation to everyone to tour the open road because as you may or may not know, Life is a Bike. You may ask, what exactly does this mean? How can life as we know it be compared to an inanimate, two-wheeled form of transportation?

As cyclists know, biking takes balance. So does life. Cycling means forward motion. Life goes forward and onward. When out on the road, cyclists encounter hills, detours, friends and foes. Sometimes we pedal hard and other times we coast. But we're ever mindful that biking exists in the moment – and that's exactly what life should be to each of us.

I, Gianna, invite you to take a spin with me. Let us tour the open road together and embrace a gamut of experiences all linked to the metaphor of bicycling. We'll explore the many aspects of life, be it traffic, hidden vistas, songbirds, libraries, whatever, wherever . . . the list just goes and grows. This is going to be gritty and delightful. Are you coming?

And what better opportunity than now to review the Laws of Bicycling? Dust off your helmet, pump up those tires and read this before you take to the road. But I think it is only fair to warn you that these aren't typical road rules. Bicycle laws defy nature and reason, so don't even attempt to prove or disprove their validity. Some things must simply be accepted on face value.

First Law of Bicycling
No matter which way you ride, it's uphill and against the wind.
This is how you may feel on your first ride of the new season. Not to worry. Though some of you will insist the start of your ride is always into the wind while your return ride is always against the wind. It's the law.

Second Law
No matter how far you ride, the return trip is always longer.
A valid illusion that helps to explain why the last few miles of a ride feel longer.

Third Law
It's always the rear wheel that gets the flat. (Forget those 50-50 odds.)

This is Murphy's Law of Cycling and life in general. It is always the most difficult thing to replace or fix which breaks down. Life is a struggle, so relax and enjoy it.

Fourth Law
You can never get lost while riding a bike; your ride is merely extended.

This places a different spin on a wrong or missed turn. It is this Zen bike attitude that will help you to just enjoy the moment and not fret about how much longer your ride has become. Of course this doesn't help if Laws One, Two, and Three have already surfaced.

Fifth Law
Thou shall stop at neighborhood lemonade stands.

This is a basic concept to think about the little guys in life whether whizzing on your road bike or in a town car.

Sixth Law
You always look younger on a bicycle.

Forget that anti-aging cream, your fountain of youth is on two wheels. Just ride. You're never too old to grow young.

Seventh Law
Cyclists never die, they just re-cycle.

Is this really a law? You bet. Year after year, we see the same merry faces on the road pedaling along the roadside.

Eighth Law
Thou shall not sell your bicycle for scrap metal.

If it isn't broken you don't fix it. If it's fixed you don't toss it. And if it's your bike, you never sell, tempted as you may be to do this especially when Laws One, Two, Three, and Four are active.

8½ Law
Thou shall not sleep with your neighbor's bike.

This is a joke. Sleeping with any bike is still not recommended, and especially your neighbor's.

Ninth Law
Always wear your helmet, your humor, and a smile.

It's easy to see the Life is a Bike attitude is to have fun – but make it safe fun.

Tenth Law
Remember, Life is a Bike, and laws are made to be broken.

Until next time . . .

BIKE BONDING
LIFE IS A BIKE©

By Gianna Bellofatto

*Like marriage, a solid relationship between biker and bike requires lots of trust
. . . and presents.*

"Cyclist divorces his bicycle!" Wouldn't that be an interesting headline? It appeared in the back of a little-circulated magazine not too long ago. Apparently the cyclist impulsively purchased a new bike, claimed he couldn't bond with it and now wanted out. I was so intrigued by the story that I called the editor to see if I could speak to the cyclist. He declined to speak with me. So, what I present is my personal proof positive of the phenomena of bike-bonding.

Much has been written about the significance of bonding. You hear about the special bonding among fathers and sons, and likewise between mothers and

daughters. But little if anything has been written about bike-bonding. I searched the Internet, and then called some serious cyclists for their input. Some of them suggested I call a bike shop and ask them what they thought. Eventually I realized I would have to be the pioneer in the psychology of bike-bonding.

I recall the process of bonding with my bike. It's similar to a love affair. As soon as I laid eyes on my bike, I knew it had everything I wanted. It was sleek, strong and responsive. We were a match. I sat with the bike and admired it for hours. First thing in the morning I took it for a spin. As soon as I got home from work I would take it out again. I spent most of my free time with the bike. First, it was just weekends and holidays. Now hardly a day goes by that I don't think about my bike. But I knew I had gone over the handlebars when I had my first "out of bike" experience.

There I was cranking home on the return trip of a thirty-mile ride when some strange rumblings began. At first I thought a filling in one of my teeth had picked up a radio signal. Then, I realized the noise was coming from my bicycle.

"You never take me any place special anymore. It's always the same route," I heard.

"What are you talking about? Just last week I took you to Piermont, New York." Who said that?

"But we didn't stop to get anything to eat. Noooo, it was just a quick spin and back home." Again the bike noise spoke.

"And what about how I was left stranded with two flats on one ride?" I retorted. We continued in silence for another mile when I decided to mend fences.

"Well, I just got the Vermont Cycling Tours brochure," I cooed. "I'm planning a special vacation just for the two of us."

Those were the magic words. Immediately my bike settled down and couldn't do enough for me. We climbed hills effortlessly. Coasted smoothly. Whizzed passed a traffic snarl in no time, and we still had energy to keep on rolling. What a bike!

Sure my bike and I are bonded. But it wasn't always a downhill coast. Even the best of bikes can become temperamental. Our anniversary date is rapidly approaching. What do you get a bike for an anniversary gift? Maybe I'll search the Internet, call some bike shops, talk to seasoned cyclists, here we go again . . . Life is a Bike and you got to love yours.

♿ ♿ ♿

A Bike–Illogic World
In Perfect Balance
Life is a Bike©

By Gianna Bellofatto

The relationship between gravity and cycling can be a little, well, tipsy, at times.

According to a fifth grade science teacher of mine, on the equinoxes (March 21 and September 22), at precisely 12:00 noon, an uncooked egg can be placed on a flat surface and remain perfectly balanced on its tip. The stars and planets are in a synchronous alignment. Gravity and other forces are all in symmetry, enabling this feat. There is also an equal division of daylight and darkness.

This may also be a good time to remove your kid's training wheels and balance your checkbook. It may also be the best time to have your day in court, since the scales of justice will be perfectly balanced. And while you're at it, you may want to end your diet since the scale will indicate that you have arrived at your ideal weight. Are these any more illogical than a two-hundred-pound person who maintains perfect equilibrium on a twenty-five-pound bicycle with wheels two inches wide?

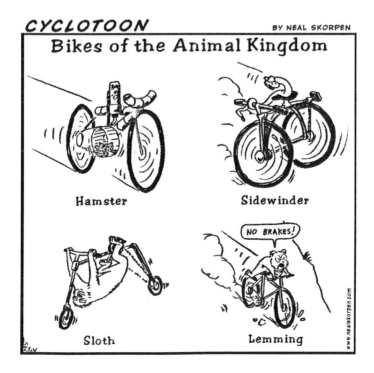

CYCLOTOON   BY NEAL SKORPEN

Bikes of the Animal Kingdom

Hamster

Sidewinder

NO BRAKES!

Sloth

Lemming

www.nealskorpen.com

It's bike-illogical. It's where the laws of gravity do not apply and properties of physics are defied. Bike-illogic is logic "stood" on its head. Which is not such an easy way to ride your bike.

Another example is June 21, known as the summer solstice or the longest day of the year – another curious concept since all days are twenty-four hours. But in the topsy-turvy world of bike-illogical, Wednesday is sundae; if you have a long weekend then Thursday becomes virtual Friday; you can spend a month of Sundays missing a loved one; while yesterday or tomorrow are both only a day away. Who cares whether the chicken or the egg came first, all I want to know is can the egg remain balanced on its tip? If you're trying to make sense of all this, it may help if you read it backwards.

This past March, I decided to test the validity and reliability of the equinox. I approached the experiment like a scientist. I checked my watch. I removed one uncooked white egg from a clear plastic bag. Held it between my thumb and forefinger. At precisely 12:00 noon I attempted to balance it on my desk at work.

The moment I released the egg chaos followed: The phone rang; then a package was delivered which I had to sign for; a colleague burst in to see if I was ready for lunch, and her son who was visiting inquired why an egg was rolling off my desk . . . splat.

🚲 🚲 🚲

In the world of bike-illogic, the elegance of physical, mental, and spiritual balance is experienced from the saddle whether it's March, September, May Day or your Aunt Tillie's birthday. Any day is a great day to put this to the test. Wide wheels or road wheels, makes no matter. All that is required are two bike wheels where the rubber meets the road. It's an ideal mixture of man, machine and the natural environment brought together in perfect harmony. The scientific explanation of how we remain balanced on a bicycle is another topic in itself, well worth exploring another time. In the meantime, it makes perfect sense that Life is a Bike.

FACTOID: DOGS CHASE BIKERS...

THE REASON ?— THEY WANT THE BIKE !

ARE YOU A GEARHEAD?

By Alan Ira Fleischmann

Denial is a deep river, my friend.
Stand tall beside that repair stand and proudly proclaim the truth!

What's your seat tube angle, 72 degrees or 73.5 degrees, and does it matter? What's your gear cluster range, 11/21 or 12/28? Is the middle ring of your "triple" a 38 or 40? What's the "Micro Drive" concept? How much trail does your fork have, and do you wish it was less (more)? If you can rattle off the answers to all of the above, then you, too, may be a "gearhead."

A gearhead, to the cycling community, is the functional equivalent of a "nerd" in high school. You remember, the geeky kid with the pocket protector who belonged to the chess club and who knew how to run the AV equipment. Well, we've given up chess and we've lost our pocket protectors. We're all grown up now, and we can fix our own bikes.

BONKERZ CARTOONS OF THE DELAWARE VALLEY BICYCLE CLUB

Still not sure about yourself? Perhaps you're still a borderline gearhead, a closet gearhead, a gearhead wannabe, or just a G.I.T. (Gearhead-In-Training)? Remember, gearheads:

+ True their own wheels and install new tires and tubes annually.

+ Adjust and lube their own headsets, derailleurs, brakes, and cables.

+ Never cycle wearing "street" clothes.

+ Have cadence sensors and heart rate monitors.

+ Have archived every issue of *Bicycling, Bicycle Guide,* and maybe even *VeloNews.*

+ Know the difference between Titanium and CroMo, Gore-Tex and Supplex, clincher and tubular, index and friction, Clip-on and Drop-in, Schrader and Presta, PSI and TPI, round and Bio-Pace, clips and cleats, STI and Ergo.

+ Spend hours perusing every issue of Performance, Nashbar, and Colorado Cyclist catalogs.

+ Have pictures of bike heroes on the wall of their offices.

+ Can program their own digital cameras, TiVo's and other assorted gadgets.

If you, too, are a gearhead, but are in denial, maybe you can try GA (Gearheads Anonymous). Each meeting begins with someone standing and proclaiming, "I am a gearhead!"

🚲 🚲 🚲

VACATION SURVIVAL FOR BIKE MANIACS WHO TRAVEL WITH NON-BIKERS

By Jay T. McCamic

Vacationing in "mixed company" can be hazardous to your fun, so arm yourself with this five-point plan, which comes to you courtesy of a "certified bike maniac."

You may know the scenario: Spouse "gearhead" is a bike freak and can blissfully ride for as long as weather and body power will hold out. If not riding, checking out bike shops can fill the rainy hours.

Spouse "non-gearhead" thinks all this is relatively amusing at home but, "Hey buddy, we are on vacation and it is time for family time." Oh boy, we got problems.

Maybe some kids are into biking while others detest the whole idea of sweating. Maybe mom wants to cuddle up with the latest Grisham novel sitting at the beach lathered up like a brown 'n' serve Thanksgiving turkey. Maybe the big event in her vacation fantasy is a visit to the teddy bear museum.

Maybe you are spending the week in East Overshoe, Nebraska, visiting your in-laws. You can't figure out for the life of you how these people were responsible for producing your wonderful spouse because their life revolves around *TV Guide* schedules and sales at the mall and where can you get the best price on kielbasa. Remember, "If you're going to be a bike maniac you got to be a bike maniac from your first metric century to your last dying day."

1. **Take your bike.** Sounds obvious, but how often have you said, "Hey, we are going to Myrtle Beach. The place has more road traffic than Manhattan on Garibaldi Day, the salt and sand aren't exactly great for my pride and joy road machine, and the whole bike rack gig is a hassle . . . the heck with it." Even better, if you can, borrow and bring an extra bike and helmet. I convinced one of my brothers-in-law to go on some extended rides when we met at Myrtle Beach one year.

2. **Do serious map and other reconnaissance.** You know your highway map isn't going to cut it, but purchasing the necessary small scale maps or guidebooks is both expensive and real "hit or miss." (Case in point: Pretend you are not from the Wheeling, West Virginia area and try to find detailed info about the River Trail or any local bike riding info. We note that the West Virginia State tourist stops have very little info on Wheeling at all and zip about Wheeling biking or Wheeling bike trails.) Bookstores sometimes offer guidebooks but they can be expensive and out of date by the time they are printed. The Internet can help with bike club contacts, but often web pages are also out of date. Mapquest, Google or other Internet mapping sites are great for highly urbanized areas but

they can sometimes be woefully inaccurate in more rural, less populated areas. (I checked out my own rural area and the roads were not accurate at all.) The best bet is still the old-fashioned way: go to the local library. Every county has one. Stop in the county seat and ask around (you need to get out of the car anyway). Non-gearheads can look up the *Complete Book of Teddy Bears* while you go to the map section and usually find a detailed county map to photocopy. Ask the research person at the desk about local bike clubs and check the library catalog for any regional guides, then scope out the yellow pages for bike shops in the area, and don't forget the community bulletin board. It is really about people. The other thing about the library method is the folks there know everyone in town and they also are in the business of finding the answer. They are not in the business of selling you something. On occasion they have called the local bike expert, club leader, etc. for me and said, "We have a guy here who wants some biking information – can you help him?" I have gotten a riding partner for the area that way.

3. **If you are not a morning person you must become one.** This is painful for some but an absolute truth. You know why. You and the gearheads of the family can set the alarm and Mr. Coffee and get out the door for some serious riding and still get back and join the rest of the gang for that necessary trip to the teddy bear museum. Or have them meet you with the car at the next cultural experience.

4. **Reject the standard American notions of cleanliness.** Scientific evidence indicates that the human body functions remarkably well without a daily twenty-minute shower complete with shampoo. Ride your bike early and meet the gang with the car at McDonald's or other fast food chain store nearest the teddy bear museum and if you are really stinky, then do a serious wash-up and change of clothes in the restroom. If all this embarrasses you, explain in your best fake foreign accent to the wide-eyed little old lady from Duluth that you are with the Ukrainian National Team, or some other gibberish. You are never going to see her again anyway.

5. **Take a large seat bag, rack pack or fanny pack.** You may want to pack stuff you never take along on rides at home, like a camera, sunscreen, pen and small notepad, pocket knife for cutting up fruit purchased at roadside stands, sandals, shirt, and cable with lock, or you can make use of the extra space to be a real hero. Say you are having such a good ride you come back to your in-laws an hour late and they're all giving you dirty looks and tapping their feet waiting to get going to the teddy bear museum. You then whip out the contents of your bike bag, which could have all sorts of goodies. You say: "Look honey, just twenty-five miles from East Overshoe on backroad 238 I found this really neat Thai restaurant that got five stars according to an article I saw posted on the wall. Here's their take-out menu." (Believe me, your in-laws will either have never heard of it or they've heard of it but have permanently deleted it from their gastronomic data banks because it doesn't serve kielbasa.) Or, "Check this out, darling, a brochure, and would you believe it, there's a new teddy bear museum in the next town over that has a special collection of bears made in Uzbekistan. Your favorite kind!" You get the idea.

᚛ ᚛ ᚛

SAFETY BIKE:
THREE CENTURIES OF SERVICE

By Mason St. Clair

Mr. St. Clair is the editor and founder of the long-running Wire Donkey Bike Zine, *a unique cycling newsletter, a.k.a. a zine, published in Nashville, Tennessee, and full of original essays, commentary, cartoons, cycling tips and other neat stuff. It is a friendly forum of camaraderie among subscribers, also known as members of "The Big Red Barn."*

Mason explains the title of the poem: "Safety bike is probably an archaic term, but refers to a bike with equal-size front and rear wheels. It is referred to as a safety bike, as compared to the 'high wheeler', which was a short-lived bike and was rather unsafe."

Safety Bike
None's your like —
Three centuries you've served!
Save a hike
Down the pike
Whether straight or curved!
Beast of wire
You require
No Mid East Oil or OPEC whim!
Inflate a tire
Light my fire
And keep my physique trim!
Diamond frame
Still the same
Down to each spoke and rim!
Work of art
Every part
We dedicate to you this hymn!

For information on subscribing to the Wire Donkey Bike Zine, *contact Mason at Masonbike@aol.com.*

⚲ ⚲ ⚲

OF DOGS AND CYCLISTS:
THE DIFFERENCE BETWEEN RIDERS

By Jill Homer

The author's observations are not so — ahem — far-fetched in this doggone astute piece.

I have always thought of myself as a cycle "tourist" – someone who uses a bicycle as a means of travel, escape and relaxation. As such, I often find myself sweating up a challenging stretch of road near my home known as Middle Canyon. The reward is a sublimely tear-jerking descent.

From time to time I see Greg pounding up the canyon. Greg is a self-proclaimed roadie who enters races and rides Middle Canyon – not so much for the alpine scenery, and not so much for the screaming descent – but to time himself on the punishing four-mile, 1,900-foot climb. Riding with Greg in Middle Canyon usually involves him approaching me from behind, nodding a quick hello, followed by several miles of me trying, rather futilely, to catch up. Despite my sluggishness, Greg told me he still enjoys my company as a fellow "roadie." In an effort to recapture my self-dignity, I always silently maintain my independence as a "tourist."

Then one evening Greg passed me as we rode by a dilapidated RV parked next to a cluster of roadside picnic tables. The campsite seemed only to be inhabited by a scrawny yellow dog, which immediately bolted for our ankles. Greg took off in a flash, leaving me, the slow cyclist, behind to deal with the dog. Amidst my shouts of fear masked by indignation, the dog, predictably, got bored and walked away.

"See, that's what separates you roadies from the rest of us," I panted at Greg, when I raced to catch up with him several hundred feet up the road. "You guys outrun the mean dogs. We usually just continue along, and if the dogs get too close for comfort, we kick the living daylights out of their ugly faces."

"Don't you think you'll get bitten?" Greg asked.

I thought about it for a second. "Probably."

"You're messing with me," he grinned, and his teeth seemed to reflect the shimmering white on his jersey. "There's no real difference between you and me." Greg gestured at my bicycle, a 2004 IBEX Corrida that was decidedly "road" in appearance. "You're just slower."

I smiled. True, Greg and I were both on skinny tires. Greg and I both had the telltale farmer tans and grease-stained hands that come of regular riding. But standing next to Greg with his sleek, streamlined helmet and skin-tight Lycra, and myself a picture of cycle frumpiness in running shorts and an *I Climbed Mt. Whitney* T-shirt, I struggled to see much similarity at all.

As he shot ahead I continued to labor up the mountain. "Greg and I might not be so different," I thought, "but we're not so much the same." I pictured that snarling yellow dog.

See, cyclists are a lot like dogs. No, not because they eat protein snacks and bark at cars. They're like dogs in that they come in different breeds, but in the end, they're all cyclists.

First there are commuters. Commuters are the Labrador retrievers of the pack. Throw them a good bicycle route, and they'll keep coming back. They love a good game of "catch" – that is, they race to catch green lights. They're highly sociable, largely domesticated and don't mind being leashed to the same roads day after day.

Then there are the recreational riders, who resemble toy poodles in that they're mostly out there for show. They often have the best bikes on the block, but those bikes only see the light of day once or twice a year. They coast gingerly along smooth payment, chrome sparkling in the sunlight, all the while smiling dreamily to grab the attention of passersby.

In contrast, there are the extreme mountain bikers, the huskies, pulling their powerful bodies over terrain that evolution never intended them to cross. Their bikes show the marks of a life fully lived, coated in mud and marred by deep scars. They live on the cusp between tame and wild, fully prepared for the roughest conditions. They work well in groups but their minds stay fiercely independent, and they're never fully content when they come down from the mountain.

Recreational mountain bikers are golden retrievers. Like their husky brothers, they love going on long rides in the mountains, jumping in the mud, and summoning their maximum energy level whenever they go out. However, they're also just as happy to curl up on the couch when the weather gets bad.

There are club riders, the Shetland sheepdogs, who are happiest in large groups. They're always nipping at the heels of other riders to keep a good drafting speed as they move in formation along the road, and they cringe at the sight of stragglers.

Road racers, on the other hand, break out of the pack when it really matters. Like greyhounds, they move in graceful unity until the time comes to rush forward in a stunning burst of speed. Their sleek, Lycra-clad bodies were built for speed, and speed alone. They can be a delicate breed, prone to freezing in the winter and unable to carry the weight of life's necessities on their ultra-light bikes.

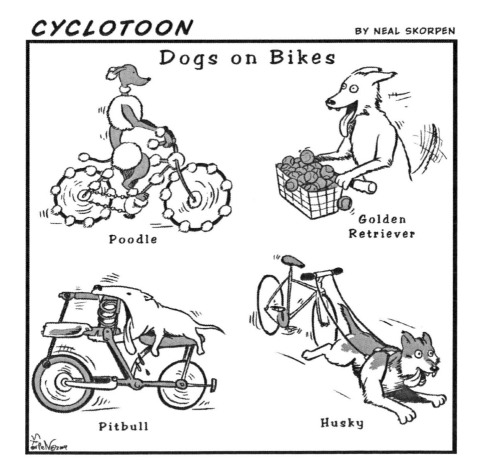

CYCLOTOON
BY NEAL SKORPEN

Dogs on Bikes

Poodle

Golden Retriever

Pitbull

Husky

That's where cycle tourists are different, and, thinking of Greg, we're vastly different. Tourists are more similar to Saint Bernards than any other breed – big, bulky, slow, but built to last, built to withstand the rain and snow and ice and wind that gets in the way during the long haul. Tourists are well adept to carrying large loads on their bikes, pulling them when necessary, moving at a steady speed until they reach their final destination, whether it's five or five-thousand miles away.

I laughed at the thought of a Saint Bernard running up a dog racing track, lumbering alongside and tripping over the greyhounds. Greg was much too far up the canyon now for me to share my scenario, and the sunlight set low on the horizon. I opted to turn my bike around, adjusted my helmet and began cranking up the gears. Soon I was moving so fast I scarcely noticed the stifled barking of the yellow dog. "We're not so different, you and me," I thought, and continued down the canyon.

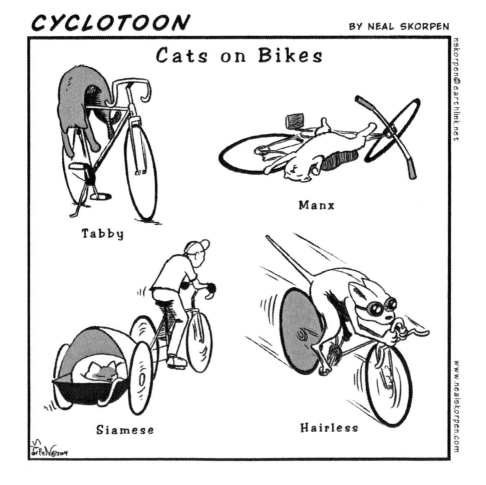

CYCLOTOON
BY NEAL SKORPEN

WISDOM

When I see an adult on a bicycle,
I do not despair for the future of the human race.

— H.G. Wells

BONKERZ

BOB LADREW © 2001

A Perfect Bike World
Life is a Bike©

By Gianna Bellofatto

In an imperfect world, one activity comes pretty darn close to perfection.

In the best of all possible worlds, bicycles would be allowed on the road and cars relegated to the shoulder lane. There would be bike lanes for ATM machines, fast food eateries, and tollbooths. Tollbooths? Ample parking would be available for bikes at all public places. One day each week would be designated for cycling only. While rewriting road rules we may as well add to our wish list, bikers need not stop at every neighborhood lemonade stand.

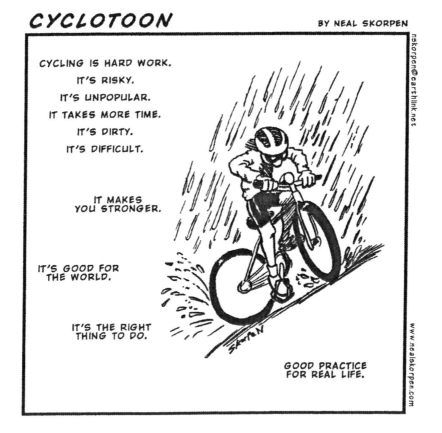

CYCLOTOON   BY NEAL SKORPEN

CYCLING IS HARD WORK.
IT'S RISKY.
IT'S UNPOPULAR.
IT TAKES MORE TIME.
IT'S DIRTY.
IT'S DIFFICULT.

IT MAKES YOU STRONGER.

IT'S GOOD FOR THE WORLD.

IT'S THE RIGHT THING TO DO.

GOOD PRACTICE FOR REAL LIFE.

nskorpen@earthlink.net

www.nealskorpen.com

We cyclists tend to be simple and virtuous folk. When has a biker been found guilty of polluting, wasting fuel, road rage, speeding, making unsolicited remarks to pedestrians, CWI (cycling while intoxicated), possessing an outdated bumper sticker, or rubber necking? We're EEE-Z. Just give us the open road and the wind at our backs. Of course, in this perfect bicycle world there would exist excellent road conditions. No potholes or sewer grates in the wrong direction. Small animals would never dart in our path, and there would be no discourteous drivers or fumes bellowing from buses. Each ride would be a serene pleasure of blue skies, songbirds, rolling hills and smooth roads.

Control-Alt-Delete. Let's reboot and look at this virtual reality with our eyes open. . . .

You're on the bike. There are cars all around coming from every direction. The road is also shared with joggers, pedestrians and squirrels. The "fresh air" is a mix of car emissions and high humidity. You just missed your turn and decide to take a side street you've never been on before and encounter a hill. Oh, boy, it looks as if it may rain soon. Get the picture? You can translate this scenario to your workplace or your home. Nothing is faultless.

Alas, when things cannot be perfect, the perfect solution is a bike attitude, where nearly every life situation can have a positive plan. It's just a matter of perspective.

From the saddle every turn becomes an adventure, every untraveled road beckons, and every bump in the road keeps you in the moment.

Even under gray skies or uncomfortable temperatures, the bike attitude is the right attitude. Cyclists embrace the unknown ride. And despite its imperfections, one should face the uncertainty of life with the same enthusiasm.

One year, I happened upon a cycling event in Westwood, New Jersey. It was sponsored by Albert's Cycle. On a whim, I decided to enter the women's race.

There I was, dressed in a plain T-shirt, tennis sneakers and shorts. I competed against women twenty years my junior who had trained months for the event. I had everything going against me, except the bike attitude. Winning wasn't my goal, however. I completed the race of twelve laps at .8 miles per lap. I came in fifth! By the way, did I mention there were only five of us in the race? Hey, no one is perfect.

Even in the perfect bike world, it's not whether I won or lost, just being there was all the fun. In the best of all possible worlds Life is a Bike.

🚲 🚲 🚲

JOY RIDE
LIFE IS A BIKE©

By Gianna Bellofatto

When I am on my bike there are no Monday mornings, my apartment is spotless, and everything is right with the world. I am Don Quixote and Huckleberry Finn all in one. I can dream the impossible dream, right every wrong, and search for adventure. I am the master of my own destiny and no destination requires waiting in line, taking a number or making a reservation. On my bike, I get the exhilaration of speed, the sun overhead and the horizon beyond. I am carefree with absolute freedom and freewheeling. I have the world by the feet and pedaling simply empowers me to a higher peace. While riding, I am young again and younger than springtime. I feel as right as rain and as fresh as morning dew.

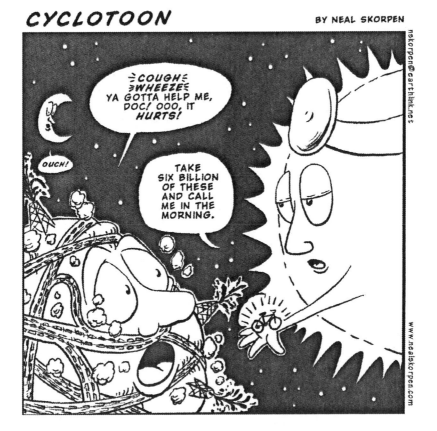

When I ride my bike the tune for the day is the whirring of the wheels. There are no bills, no meetings to attend, and all the laundry is done. On my bike, I enjoy the splash of wind in my face and the sudden jolt of a bump. There are no dinners to cook, the office work is distant, and life is in order. When I'm on my bike all my Christmas shopping is done. I have everything I want and want nothing more. On the bicycle I feel the joy of life and the ride is a joy.

Up and down hills, past parks, winding in and out of back roads, leaning into curves, these are all that is required to get a kick. When I am on my bike, I can recall every right answer, all my mistakes are pardoned, and a disparaging word exists for no one. Spinning spokes and spinning daydreams, my creativity peaks, revelations are unveiled and stories are born. I have boundless energy to do more and go further.

Speeding downhill while surroundings become blurred adds to the excitement of the moment – and every moment is accounted and embraced. When I'm on my bike the sky is a merry yellow. Whether dawn or dusk, midday, mid-week or mid-life, it's a new bright beginning. Twirling spokes breeze me to Wonderland and Oz transforming the ordinary to magic. When on my bike I don't have to grow up. I don't have to answer the phone, count my change, or make excuses. There are no ASAPs, no regrets, or RSVPs.

But when the ride ends, I am again Gianna Q. Citizen, who must pay bills, return phone calls, and do the dishes. Yet while Life is a Bike, there are no Monday mornings, my apartment is spotless . . . nothing will matter but the ride. Just ride.

⚲ ⚲ ⚲

ROMANCING THE BIKE
LIFE IS A BIKE©

By Gianna Bellofatto

Ahhh, that's amore! Where there smoke, there's spin.
There's just something about a bike.

The other day I spotted a young couple on a bike. The man pedaled as his girlfriend sat on the cross bar. His arms encircled her while he held the handlebars. It looked so charming and innocent. For an instant I forgot I was in the 21st century. But there it was, as if handed down through the ages, the familiar scene of a bicycle and two people enjoying the closeness to one another – and the danger! For romance and riding can be treacherous. Yet together they make a delicious combination that is sure to bring out the adventurous side in any of us.

Maybe it was the way her hair was loose and wind swept. Perhaps it was his open shirt and the way he leaned his face against hers. The sunlit street on a summer morning added beauty to the moment. I have no recollection about the type of bike

that they were riding. That isn't the point. They were breaking the rules! Two on a bicycle and neither was wearing a helmet. Not serious riders, I thought, but serious lovers.

It was Saturday and I was taking a short spin to a friend about nine miles south.

I daydreamed that this couple would stop in some grassy glen beneath a tree and enjoy shared summer kisses. There's nothing like a bicycle leaned against a shade tree with two forms enveloped in each other's arms to complete the scene. I never had a beau who picked me up on his bicycle and whisked me away to a quiet field on a hot summer's day. And now my cycling is with a helmet, spare tube, water bottle and lip balm.

Notice too how a bicycle is the vehicle of choice in movies when directors want to capture both romance and adventure. In *A Little Romance* and *Butch Cassidy and the Sundance Kid* lovers take a spin on a bike. In *Breaking Away* vulnerability was pivotal to the hero; and just placing a character on a bicycle riding a lonely stretch of road will surely get the viewer's heart pounding.

There is something magical about someone on a regular bike, wearing plain clothes, or perhaps riding barefoot. A couple on a bike is undeniably romantic. Their smiles and special love speak to our souls. A longing for our youth and less complicated days brims to the surface. Sure they're breaking the rules, but that's why Life is a Bike.

🚲 🚲 🚲

IT'S THE SPIN

By Alan Ira Fleischmann

Our wise sage of spin lays out the science of it in layman's terms.

Have you ever noticed that the horsepower ratings for your car are stated at a particular RPM, or engine speed? This is because any engine is more efficient at a moderately high RPM. You, as the engine of your bicycle, are too. For cycling, RPM is referred to as "cadence," or the speed at which you spin the pedals. Spin faster, and you – the engine – will be more powerful and efficient.

When you downshift your car to climb a steep hill, you're actually changing the gear ratio to allow the engine to spin faster, thereby providing more horsepower to the wheels. Most cars reach their maximum horsepower at about 5,000 RPM. Most cyclists can reach their maximum power output (one quarter to one-half horsepower) at a cadence between 85 and 100 RPM.

Maintaining a higher cycling cadence requires practice. A cycle computer also helps, but is not an absolute necessity. The general rule of thumb is that a higher cadence will provide more power while being less tiring, and causes less strain on the knees. A cadence of 90 RPM is generally considered optimal, but yours may vary depending on your own gearing, the terrain, the length of your crank arms, and your level of conditioning. Many riders use the cadence function on their cycle computers to determine when to shift up and down through the gears.

If your cadence is generally in the 60-70 RPM range (that's about one complete pedal rotation every second), try increasing it by ten to twenty per minute. Over the course of a few longer rides, you should notice a decrease in fatigue, and an increase in your power.

Another important part of the pedal stroke is the "spin." If you're simply pushing down on the pedals, you're only utilizing about forty percent of your usable power. If you have two cages or clipless pedals, you should be pulling up in the backstroke as well. Optimally, and with practice, you can train yourself to exert pressure on the pedals throughout the entire circular path of the pedals. Again, I compare the bicycle to the car engine: Simply pushing the pedals on the downstroke would be equivalent to a two-cylinder engine. Pulling on the upstroke as well increases the efficiency to that of a four-cylinder engine. Exerting pedal pressure through the entire circular stroke is the functional equivalent of an eight-cylinder engine. With the same engine sizes, an eight-cylinder engine works less, but provides more power, than one with only two cylinders.

Train your engine to be a V-8, and spin it fast!

🚲 🚲 🚲

THE PRICE OF EVERYTHING
(AND THE VALUE OF BICYCLES)

By Chip Haynes

Strengthen your portfolio. Pedal over to your local bike shop,
the best investment house in town, and ride with the bulls.

A further corruption of Oscar Wilde? I believe it is – if a further corruption of Oscar Wilde was even possible. I got to thinking about this last night on my ride home from work as I passed Davidson's. Now, I have to admit, I'm not entirely sure what it is that Davidson's actually does. It's a big aluminum warehouse/garage out on the edge of the downtown business district, and it's always just chock-full of expensive foreign cars and SUVs. I use to think it was a detail shop, but now I think they simply buy and sell pricey upscale cars.

I was thinking about the price of those cars and the price of the bike I was riding – and which was worth more. I was riding my fixed gear bike. I know I built it for cheap, but the replacement costs would be considerably higher. I figure you could duplicate my bike for about $1,000, or roughly fifty dollars a pound. Fifty dollars a pound? Hmmm . . . how (I wondered) does that compare to all of those shiny cars?

Let's say you spend $30,000 for a nice car that weighs, oh, let's say 3,000 pounds. Not heavy, but not really light, either. Ten dollars a pound – not all that expensive by today's standards. Of course, if that's a Porsche, you'll be spending twenty dollars

a pound, minimum. Looking for a car at fifty dollars a pound? Now you're talking Ferrari, and that does come closer in concept to a hand-built bike in its inherent value, if not actual craftsmanship.

"By the pound" is an interesting way to look at the things we have. My Raleigh folder was an absolute bargain at about two dollars a pound. What a deal! (Okay, so it's a heavy bike I bought at the pawnshop – what's your point?)

Is this a good way to price stuff you don't eat? Probably not, but it sure is fun. Fun, but lacking, and what's lacking is the element of time. A car is generally worth less over time but, if it lasts long enough, it starts to regain value as a collectible antique. Unless it's a Pinto, of course.

Less expensive bicycles suffer that fate as well, but high-end bikes, like high-end cars, do not. Fine bikes, like Rivendells, Jacksons and Colnagos, will never be worth less than what they went for new. Why? Because good bikes don't age. They never go out of style and, quite literally, don't seem to wear out. My Bob Jackson will soon be thirty years old, and it's still the sleek ready-to-go-anywhere touring bike I bought new back in 1975. Can we say the same of a 1975 Ferrari 365 GTB/4 Daytona? I'm not sure. I'll stick with the Jackson, at only thirty-two dollars a pound. (And those are 1975 dollars, of course.)

When it comes to price and value, the good bicycle wins out every time over the car – any car. It will last longer and ride better with less fuss than any motored machine. It will hold its value and keep its good looks for as long as you own it, assuming you're not a complete jerk about it.

Fifty dollars a pound for a bicycle? Such a bargain. What a deal! You just don't find value like that anymore. Well, not in the car dealers' showrooms, anyway. In all honesty, I probably have less than $300 in that fixed gear bike – so that really is a great deal. I guess that's why I always feel so smug when I pedal past Davidson's. I know I've got the best deal on wheels, worth its weight in gold.

ᚁᚂ ᚁᚂ ᚁᚂ

It's All Right To Ride Upright:
An ode to the mountain bike and the railbed trail

By James Brink

A roadie discovers there's more to life than just skinny tires. . . .

Okay, so I am a traditionalist. I admit that I am still wearing my circa 1978 Detto Article 74 shoes. The only change made from the original, other than to re-stitch the seams, was to affix Look pedal cleats where old slotted cleats were previously attached.

I also submit that I must be the only person left on the planet who rides a Brooks professional racing saddle; yes, the original, unpadded, hard leather version originally purchased in 1979 for my Schwinn Continental and later moved in 1982 to my Trek 620, my current steed.

Every spring I soak the underside of this saddle with neatsfoot oil and completely coat the exterior with saddle soap. This treatment makes the saddle more comfortable, at least this is what I tell myself and others.

Finally, I still believe that steel is more comfortable than aluminum and carbon fiber and I believed that true cyclists ride bent over and "in the drops."

It was with great skepticism that I greeted the sudden and intense interest in mountain bikes, a.k.a. all-terrain bicycles (ATBs). I can remember back in the '80s, *Bicycling Magazine* sponsoring a contest to name this new-fashioned machine. I can't remember the entries, but mountain bike must have been the winner.

What bothered me the most about these new bikes was the riding position of the riders. They sat upright. Through my cynical eyes they looked liked Elvira Gulch going after Toto right before the big storm. They reminded me of the faded sepia tintypes of the first cyclists of the Gay '90s (the 1890s, that is).

The true cyclists regarded the new bikes as a fad and summarily dismissed them. This is the same group of true cyclists who also saw Madonna perform on a New Year's Eve special in 1984 and rendered the same opinion.

We were wrong on both counts.

I watched the new sport develop until 1994, and then I could wait no longer. I acquired my own mountain bike. But before I could bring myself to ride my new bike, I raised the seat and lowered the handlebars, which were already attached to a moderately-extended stem. I took a bike that was designed to seat the rider in an upright position and managed to force a semblance of the classic crouch.

Since my new acquisition was actually a Christmas gift, I bundled up in ski clothes, loaded my new machine on the rack and set out for the Montour Trail (www.montourtrail.org), an abandoned railbed converted to a multi-purpose trail outside of Pittsburgh. I was hooked at once.

Before long, I realized that a whole new world of cycling had opened. No longer would I be tied to the thin strip of asphalt granted to me by my four-wheeled brethren of the road. I could actually ride without constantly listening for the humming of upcoming tires behind me or looking over my left shoulder for a lumbering four-wheel drive fueled by a six-pack of Bud Light. Mountain biking was so quiet and stress free. I could ride twenty-eight miles one way and cross only a handful of roads and driveways. This was cycling at its best. Within a year I reached the point that ninety percent of my cycling was done on my mountain bike on the Montour Trail.

I learned about other trails from my cycling contacts. The Yough River Trail (YRT) extends two ways out of Ohiopyle State Park in the beautiful Laurel Highlands, of Fallingwater fame. It's one of the most peaceful bike rides ever experienced. With a few short detours, the Montour Trail connects via the Steel Valley Trail with the YRT, which extends in a winding southeastern direction to the head of the C & O Canal Towpath in Cumberland, Maryland. (The entire 150-mile trail system between Pittsburgh and Cumberland has been christened,

"The Great Allegheny Passage." For detailed interactive maps and information, visit www.greatalleghenypassage.org.) From Cumberland one can ride the old canal towpath 185 miles into the heart of Washington, DC.

I took a memorable ride on this trail one weekend following several days of heavy rain. All along the uphill side of the trail and down through the valleys to the Youghiogheny River were hundreds of cascading waterfalls. I could not help but stop every fifty feet or so to look.

I could go on forever about my bucolic railbed biking experiences. Maybe another time. For now, however, I must report for the more technical readers that I discovered there are definite physical benefits to riding a thirty-pound mountain bike. In contrast, my twenty-three-pound road bike disappeared from beneath me. Its sleekness, weight, and low rolling resistance made pedaling effortless after pushing knobbies in crushed gravel.

A word of advice to neophyte converts: I became so enamored with my mountain bike and so overly confident in my physical condition that I attempted a short, thirty-five-mile road ride with an organized group of road riders. Big mistake, even after a 1,000-mile summer.

I found that I could not keep up with the riders on traditional road bikes. While I was able to gear down for the hills, I was unable to coast down the back and regain my strength. I about bonked on a normally easy ride. Never again. The mountain bike will forever stay where it was meant to stay.

That is just fine for me because of the large number of railbed trails in Western Pennsylvania and West Virginia. The final analysis from this "true cyclist" is that it is all right to ride upright – sometimes.

๑๖ ๑๖ ๑๖

BITS 'N BOLTS FROM *ASK THE MECHANIC*

Excerpts from "Andy the Mechanic" Wallen's
Bike Repair Column on Bikexchange.com

Since the September 1996 launch of Bikexchange.com a.k.a. The Bicycle Exchange, Andy Wallen has fielded bicycle fix-it questions from around the world. Below is a selection of ten general Q & A's from Andy's column. With no baloney, Andy tells it like it is . . .

Be Wise and Try It Out For Size

Andy,

I would like to get a new road bike and am unsure about what dimensions I should look for. I am 6' 2" tall and do occasional rides of fifty miles at a leisurely pace — I'm not a racer. I don't have a whole lot of money to spend since I'm raising two sons that suck the money out of me. I do, however, like to ride. I would like to know what I am looking for as much as possible before I go and purchase the wrong cycle.

Presently I have a Schwinn Guadalupe road bike and I am having trouble finding parts for it. It's an old bike but has served me well. Any advice?

Thanks,
Mark

DINNER WITH BIFF

(ANOTHER SIGN THAT BIKING IS TAKING OVER HIS LIFE)

Mark,

Getting a bike to fit requires more than just your height. It is not likely that a good fit can be achieved without going to a shop and at least trying two or three different frames. All brands are not the same – you may like the standover height on a 62 cm Brand X, but the top tube might be too short. Stems, seatposts, and handlebars can be changed, but the basic frame fit is still critical. Also, keep in mind that while one can buy a fairly nice all-terrain bike for around $600, even Taiwanese road bikes are much more than that at entry level. Beware of those "made in USA of foreign and domestic parts" frames, as these are usually of Asian origin (stuffed into a box in the USA). Usually, a person of your size can find a good price on a close-out bike, as most manufacturers sell out of 52-58 cm frames, but often have leftovers in the 48, 50, 60, and 62 sizes.

Good luck,
Andy

His Aching Back!

Hi Andy,

I am relatively new to cycling (five months) but have been hitting it hard. I have been riding road bikes (an older Peugeot and now an older Trek). Both of them have given me an ache in the lower back after thirty to forty miles. Is this normal, or is there a seat or handle bar adjustment that I am missing? Seems like I have tried a lot of different combinations. Both bikes have had the downswept road bike-style handlebars.

Thank you,
Dennis

Dennis,

Physiology is not my area of expertise, but here is two cents worth:

1) Include stretches that involve the affected area in your pre- and post-ride stretch routines.

2) Use the off-season to strengthen the lower back muscles. Start a weight program and/or an ab and back exercise routine. Crunches and lat pulls really help, and anything you can do to work the upper body contributes to effective cycling and overall fitness. It's possible that your "older" bikes have short top tubes, which don't allow enough room for a more comfortable position, but if you've tried different stems and such, the problem could be your body, not the bike.

Andy

The Debate From Hell: Campy vs. Shimano

Andy,

What's your opinion of Campagnolo vs. Shimano and what are the pros and cons of these two component groups?

Mike

Mike,

You are probably after an unbiased objective opinion, so here it is. I appreciate the Old World appeal and high quality of most Campy parts. If you buy Record stuff (or Chorus), it will probably outlast your frame. But – who wants to hang on to stuff forever, when technology moves at the speed of light? Some folks do. Most of us want the newest and slickest stuff, so why spend more on Campy stuff if you plan to dump (I mean upgrade) it every year or two? Probably the biggest downside to Campy is that it is not universal, nor is any part of the shift system Shimano compatible. You can buy Shimano cassettes, hubs, wheelsets anywhere in the world; I would speculate that most American bike shops have very limited Campy inventory – I don't have any.

Love 'em or hate 'em, Shimano wins for practicality.

Andy

Aye, Ya Salty Dog

Andy,

Will road salt affect my aluminum frame, especially where the paint is rubbed off?

Michael

Michael,

My educated guess is that since salt is a corrosive, and since aluminum does "rust" (you can say that it oxidizes or some other euphemism, but, in truth, it rots, just like anything else), then any corrosive will accelerate the rusting action. (This is not as obvious as what happens to your '73 Pinto after a few northern West Virginia winters, but is probably somewhat dangerous in a sneaky sort of way.)

Many factors contribute to the breakdown of an aluminum frame. Any one of these factors, and I would include corrosion, could cause an imperceptible crack to develop. Cyclical fatigue can turn these little cracks into catastrophic failures rather quickly. My rule, which everyone is too cheap to follow, is to replace aluminum ATB frames every five years, and road frames every eight. If either was crashed, regardless of the lack of any apparent damage, replace it. If your paint is bubbling up because of corrosion, I would replace the frame rather than risk death or injury.

Andy

P.S. On the sales floor, we often hear from "Joe the Know-It-All Mountain Biker" – who rode in a race once – and says to buy an aluminum frame because it won't rust and will therefore outlast steel. While it is true that the type of breakdown that generally occurs in a twenty-year-old, abused steel frame is not as obvious in aluminum, aluminum is prone to cyclical failures, corrosion, and once bent it should never be straightened.

Coasting Along

Andy,

I just bought a secondhand Pinarello with Dura-Ace & Ultegra 600 components. I love it. However, in recent races I've noticed that other people starting at the top of a hill at the same speed can coast faster than me and accelerate past me without pedaling. The bearings and brakes do not seem to be binding although I have not repacked them. Any suggestions?

Richard

Richard,

Coasting is one of those things that can be influenced by several physical and mechanical variables. To make a valid comparison, you must ride the exact same hill under the exact same conditions on two different bikes. Assuming you have done this, we can address issues such as bearing/grease in the wheels, width and air pressure in the tires (skinnier + higher pressure = faster), handlebar width/positioning (narrower + lower = faster), bike and/or wheel weight. Light wheels have only one downside: They usually don't roll as fast downhill. It's a simple question of momentum, once you get a higher mass in motion, that higher mass has more potential inertia. This applies to the mass of the entire bike and rider as well. So if your bearings are good, you ride in the same aerodynamic tuck as your friends, etc.

Maybe it's light wheels/tires, or maybe you need to put on a few pounds. Fat guys on cheap bikes can just fly down hills. This is one reason spoked-molded wheels are so popular (Spin, Spinergy, etc.). Most of them are considerably heavier than good wire-spoked wheels, but the combination of aerodynamics and added rotational inertia make them seem very fast, and they are, unless you're climbing.

Andy

Little Sophistication to Proper Chain Lubrication

Andy,

A lot has been written about chain maintenance. My own experience is rather weird.

I came to the conclusion that it doesn't much matter which lubricant one uses. I've tried sewing machine oil, semi-fluid lube oil for automatic weapons, old motor oil, motorcycle chain oil – all working okay. The only lousy product I ever used was Finish Line KryTech chain wax lubricant but, anyway, I can't afford it now.

The only thing that seems important to me is that one lubes the chain after all. Is this also your experience?

Regards,
Martin

Martin,

It is better to put hair tonic or bear grease on your chain than it is to let it rust. Unless you are collecting samples of all the dust, dirt, feathers, hair, and insects that you ride through on a given day, you might want to consider using a bike-specific lube. Some people would rather spend time looking for alternatives to something that is already rather inexpensive and widely available, but it doesn't make sense to use anything not designated for bicycle chains. Triflow is very cheap and works well. I can understand one's hesitancy regarding expensive miracle lubes, but all chain lubes do not fall into this category.

Andy

Andy's Classroom Lesson On Gears and Changing Speeds

Hi! My name's Michelle and I'm doing a paper for school on gears and changing speeds. Could you tell me a little about this subject? It would be a great help!

Michelle

Michelle,

Here is an overview. The standard mountain bike has three chainrings (also called chainwheels or sprockets) in the front and eight or nine cogs in the back. Road bikes usually have two chainrings and eight, nine, or ten cogs, but some of them have three chainrings. Simply stated, you have what we call "big" gears and "little" gears. Big gears go fast, and little gears climb hills. On a standard road bike with two chainrings and nine cogs, your biggest gear happens when you put the chain on the biggest chainring and the smallest cog. This gear is best referred to by the number of teeth on the chainring followed by the number of teeth on the cog, or 53/12. This is the fastest gear on the bike, because a single revolution of the chainring produces several (I'm not going into the physics of the thing here – to be exact, you'd need to count wheel rollouts, or perhaps your physics teacher could devise a formula) revolutions of the rear wheel. Conversely, the little gear happens when the chain is on the smallest chainring and biggest cog (usually 39/23 on road bikes), and this is the easiest gear to climb hills with, because a single revolution of the chainring produces something close to a single revolution of the rear wheel.

If you had a bike with only three chainrings (20-30-40) and three cogs (10-20-30), and no wheel size involved, you could devise gear ratios, like 20/20=1:1; 20/30=2:3, etc. Bicycle people have devised a system for comparing gears called gear inches. To determine gear inches, you multiply the tire size in inches by the number of chainring teeth and divide by the number of cog teeth. While it is erroneous to use this number as a representation of a physical event, it is useful in that you can use the gear inch number, like 52 or 26, to compare gear changes on different-sized wheels, or to better understand the difference in changing cog or chainring sizes.

Hope this helps,
Andy

Andy's Step-By-Step Guide to Getting Rid of Clunking Gear Changes

Hi, I need some pointers to solve a problem that has developed with the rear derailleur on my wife's touring bike. It shifts up fine. When shifting from larger to smaller gear cogs, though, it clunks into gear. I've eyeballed the effect carefully and it appears as though instead of the chain engaging the gear cogs one link at a time, it rides on top of them and then engages all the links at once. The effect when riding is both the "clunk" plus – more worrisome – some free travel in the pedal crank as the chain skips forward slightly until the links slot on to the gear cog. If I'm pushing uphill at the time this is both scary and dangerous.

I've had the wheel apart to check it out – all the gear teeth look fine and the freewheel runs smoothly.

I'm perplexed and am now about to resort to the desperate measure of cleaning the chain. I've searched the Net and not found anyone describing a similar problem.

Any pointers?

Thanks,
Bruce

Bruce,
If you have a Suntour drivetrain, you can't fix it. If you have a Shimano drivetrain, check the following, in this order:
1. Cable and housing should be clean, lubed, no kinks in housing.
2. Measure chain for wear. If it has elongated links, replace the chain and cassette.

3. Make sure that the derailleur returns to its rested position (high gear) smoothly with the cable disconnected. You could have some obstruction, such as bent linkages or warped plastic.
4. Check the pulley wheels for worn teeth and smooth operation. The upper wheel must slide back and forth slightly as well as turn freely.
5. Make sure that the derailleur hanger is not bent inward.

Andy

The Top Ten Most Common Creaking Sources

Andy,

I have a 2002 Specialized Stumpjumper FSR XC that's creaking really bad and driving me nuts. I've determined that it's not the seat or seat post. I've taken out the bottom bracket, greased the cones and tightened them back down. I've checked the pedals. I've checked the chainring bolts. It's still creaking and driving me crazy. Any suggestions?

Thanks,
Craig

Craig,

In order of frequency, here's my list of the most common creaks:

10. Headset loose in frame.
9. Crack in frame or fork.
8. Shoes/pedals.
7. Handlebar to stem. Sometimes a little grease on the bar helps.
6. Seat rails in clamp. Grease rails, tighten clamp. Check for loose rail or crack in saddle.
5. Suspension parts – good luck here!
4. Crank spider lock nuts, or chainring bolts.
3. Wheels/skewers. Grease the skewer – all areas that contact the frame, inside and out.
2. Bottom bracket cup loose, or needs Teflon tape, especially in non-ferrous frames.
1. Crank arm too loose on tapered spindle.

Andy

Andy Shoots Straight With Teen Exploring Bike Mechanic Career

Hi, we have to do a paper on a career we would like to do after we graduate and we have to interview someone about the career. I am thinking about becoming a bike repairer and I was wondering if you could answer this list of questions for me.

Thanks,
Remington

Remington,

This is one of those jobs that you have to love. It doesn't pay well, and it's not always fun. You do get a great deal on bikes. Here you go:

1. What is your name? (name of business)
Wheelcraft, Ltd. (See www.wheelcraft.us)

2. What types of things do you do as a bike repairer?

I do everything: build bikes from scratch, assemble new bikes, wheel building, wheel trueing, lots of tire/tube repair, tune ups, frame alignment, estimates, and unfortunately, all too many Huffy/Murray/Pacific/Mongoose problems. Also, since this is a very small business, I have to sell bikes and accessories, sweep the floor, etc.

3. What is the average salary per year? (month)

I don't know the average salary, but I know that very few mechanics make over $20,000, and most shop owners don't make much more than that. Depending on where you work, business can be seasonal, so you may make $1,000 - $1,200 per month in the summer, but get laid off from October to March.

4. What hours do you work? When do you start and get off?

I work over sixty hours per week in the summer, and about forty in the winter. I start at around 9 A.M. in the summer, and leave as soon as possible, which usually turns out to be 7 P.M., and sometimes, come back after supper and work until 9:30 or 10 P.M. When we hire mechanics or assemblers, I don't expect them to work as much as I do, so they usually have a six to eight-hour day, and less than forty-hour weeks.

5. What do you like about your job? Dislike about it?

I like almost everything about my job. Most of my customers really appreciate what I do. Even though I work a lot, I feel like I have a lot of control over what I do, because I make the decision as to what gets done now, and what gets done later. Top five dislikes:

1. Mail order (and Internet) prices.
2. People who bring up #1.
3. Junk bikes (especially Pacific – this includes Mongoose and Schwinn/GT).
4. People who won't take no for an answer.
5. Not being able to ride 5,000 miles per year.

6. *Do you get paid vacation days?*

We get an all expenses paid three-day "vacation" to sunny Las Vegas every year for the Interbike Exhibition, and that's about it. I'm salaried, so I get paid whether I work or not, but I really don't get what you'd call a vacation.

7. *What is needed to get hired? Any college or basic training?*

You should have a degree in music education – like me – with twelve hours toward your Master's degree. Seriously, I'd try to get some training, if you can. I would much rather hire someone who completed a training program than to hire someone who just thinks they know what they're doing.

8. *Why did you choose this career?*

I chose to do this when I realized that I would never get along with any school superintendent in any district in the universe, and, by association, would never be able to do the will of anyone in any position of authority; in other words, I must be my own boss. I also love all types of cycling, and had worked in a bike shop during and after college.

9. *If you just graduated and were choosing a career, would you have still picked this?*

No. It's too hard to make a sufficient income at this job.

Andy

The bus is in the shop.

WELL HELLO THERE, ED!
(LONG SEE, NO TIME)

By Chip Haynes

He rode a bicycle — what else do you need to know?

I f you're a regular bike commuter like me, you probably take the same roads almost every day. Sure there are days when you just have to break out and go nuts, but most days, it's the same old roads the same old way. And you see the same old people (and the same young people, too.) Me, I see the same other bicycle commuters several times a week. They're going the other way on the other side of the road, so for years we've just waved at each other across the traffic. Sort of like a secret handshake, I guess.

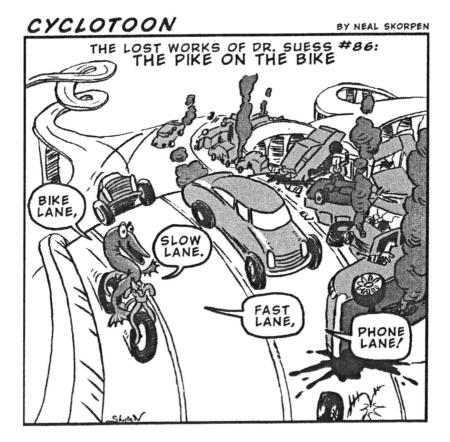

CYCLOTOON — BY NEAL SKORPEN

THE LOST WORKS OF DR. SUESS #86: THE PIKE ON THE BIKE

BIKE LANE,

SLOW LANE.

FAST LANE,

PHONE LANE!

For quite some time I've seen the same bicycle commuter on Lakeview Avenue. He is headed west – and downhill – as I head east and (you guessed it) uphill. Seemed like a nice enough guy, considering I knew absolutely nothing about him. He rode a bicycle – what else do you need to know? All of that changed yesterday as I was stopped at the side of the road, waiting for a break in traffic to cross an intersection. Here he came; we were about to meet.

He stopped and we talked like two old friends who had never met. His name was Ed. (Okay, so technically my name is Ed, too, but I didn't tell him that. He laid claim to it first, so I figured I'd let him have it.) He was riding a nice Cannondale mountain bike (Hard Tail) with street tires. Nice ride. He had it all outfitted for commuting, except no fenders. Handlebar cell phone holder, yes, but no fenders. Go figure. A front bag, lights, a frame pump – he was ready for just about anything, with the possible exception of a little rain. To each his own, I guess. But I'm glad I have fenders.

Once he took off his spiffy, sporty sunglasses, I could see that he was not as young as I had thought. (I wonder if he thought the same of me, now that he saw me up close.) He said his commute was ten miles one way, and that he really enjoyed it. He got a kick out of astounding his co-workers with the fact that he commuted that far everyday, and really enjoyed pedaling past gas stations and laughing. From the sound of it, he doesn't own a car. Good for him. He mentioned that he'd suffered a heart attack a while back, but had been cycling a bit even before that. He also explained that he had been much heavier then, and cycling had helped take the weight off – and helped keep him alive. Very good for him.

We talked about bikes and roads and cars and drivers, and it was good to hear another bicycling commuter with a positive attitude – he was happy to be cycling, and enjoyed every minute of it – even in the rain and traffic. After five minutes or so we parted ways, but now we knew each other. From now on, that wave has a name attached to it. Cool.

I've often suspected that there are far more bicycle commuters out there than I will ever see. Different roads, and different times, all conspire to hide us from each other. How could you possibly get us all together in one place? (Offering free bike tires might do it.) It would be interesting to see all of the bicycle commuters in this town in one place at one time. Until then, I guess we'll just have to meet two at a time, along the side of the road. Of course, if the oil runs out and we all ride bikes – it's a party!

⛷ ⛷ ⛷

This piece first appeared in Mason's Wire Donkey Bike Zine. *For subscription info, contact Mason St. Clair, Editor and Founder, at masonbike@aol.com.*

Snap, Rattle, Crunch, Bang!

By Chip Haynes

It doesn't take much to keep a bike running smoothly, so what's up with this guy?

I heard it coming and I had to look. From behind me on the sidewalk, he passed me, moving barely faster than I was walking: A tall, lanky guy on a red Fuji folding mountain bike. He was all hunched over the handlebars, smoking a cigarette and moving just fast enough to keep the bike balanced. Not a bad bike, but both the bike and the rider had problems.

Snap, rattle, crunch, bang!

I watched him pedal slowly away, and looked at the bike. The seat was too low. The tires were too low. The derailleurs were out of adjustment and something – either a pedal or a crank arm – was either loose or broken. Maybe both. I have a

soft spot for good bikes that are stuck with bad owners, and I wouldn't mind having one of those folding Fujis myself. I'll bet I could fix that one right up, and have it running smoothly and silently in no time at all. But it was not to be. He pedaled slowly across the intersection and down the sidewalk, as I turned into the office building and went back to work.

Snap, rattle, crunch, bang!

It was almost painful to listen. Didn't he hear it? How could he not? Did he think that's what bicycles were supposed to sound like? Or ride like? Geez Louise. People are idiots. If you go through life with that understanding, you're seldom disappointed and only occasionally surprised. That guy was an idiot, and his bicycle was suffering as a result. (So was I, just to hear it.) Not to mention, he wasn't doing much for the image of bicycling. Still, wouldn't he have been happier with a bike that was working as well as it was meant to work?

Properly set up, the bicycle is not only, as Daniel Berhman once put it, the noblest of man's inventions, it's also the most efficient. It's five times more efficient than walking. Set up correctly for its rider, the bicycle is a delight to use – fast, quiet and effortless. Do it wrong – or not at all – and it's a noisy, energy-sucking mess. Who wants that? So what happened with Sparky there?

I'm guessing he got the bike cheap or for free, and no one bothered to mention he might want to raise the seat for his six-foot-tall frame . . . or that he might need to spritz a little atmosphere into those big knobby tires every couple of weeks or so . . . or that "bang" was not, in fact, a sound a bicycle should ever make. (Not to mention snap, rattle, or crunch.) I'm really sorry I let that one get away. I should have yelled at him and offered him twenty bucks for the bike. I'll bet he would have taken it. Next time.

Bicycles don't take much to keep running, but they do take a little, every once in a while. Keep yours in tune, and it will ride forever. A little air in the tires, a spot of grease now and then, and it will do just fine. Please. Don't make me listen to that noise again.

Snap, rattle, crunch, bang!

Ugh.

🚲 🚲 🚲

This piece first appeared in Mason's Wire Donkey Bike Zine. *For subscription info, contact Mason St. Clair, Editor and Founder, at masonbike@aol.com.*

Is Bicycling All That Bad?
You'd Rather Do This?

By Chip Haynes

It's downright crazy what some people will do for exercise.

I t was a rainy day, so JoAnn planned to drop me off at work. That changed my morning routine, and gave us both plenty of time to watch the local morning news on TV, which I don't usually do. (Whoa – would you look at all that rain on the radar!) Our morning news station tries to end their program with something a little less disturbing than the usual murder, mayhem, and political intrigue, so they have a reporter who does human interest stories to finish the show. Today's story was just annoying.

BONKERZ Cartoons of the Delaware Valley Bicycle Club

DOC, WHEN I PEDAL A BIKE MY LEGS HURT BELOW THE KNEES. WHAT'S WRONG?

YOU'VE GOT SCHWINN-SPLINTS.

BOB LADREW © 2002

The reporter had gone to a local exercise gym/spa that was featuring their idea of the latest in "fun" exercise: Playing on a big soft ball. You sat on the ball with your feet on the floor and sort of danced around like a five-year-old on a sugar high. You waved your arms and kicked your legs and bounced your bottom on the big, soft ball. In short, you looked like an idiot. I watched three alleged adults do this – on TV, for all the world to see – and I couldn't help but wonder: You'd rather do this than ride a bicycle? Are you nuts?

I know a lot of people don't ride bicycles because they think it makes them look foolish (being stuck in traffic doesn't?). These same people drive through traffic to get to the health club or gym, where they'll do all manner of foolish things in a vain attempt to "get in shape." Does it really work? Think about it: If the health club really worked all that well, they'd lose their members. They'd all be bankrupt inside of a year.

Someone needs to tell these people that all they need to do to get in shape is walk a little more and ride a bicycle. No health club dues, no fancy-schmancy equipment, no bouncing ball. No need to drive halfway across town to get in shape. Cut the travel time. Cut the crapola. Ride a bike.

Maybe we need to offer the public more dignified bikes? We need to stop pushing the brightly colored, full-zoot, 85-speed, full-suspension mountain bikes. That might help. Stop intimidating average schmoes with complex bikes they don't need. Give them a nice three-speed with a comfy seat and fenders. And would it be so bad to have a real chain guard on the thing?

While bikes are often touted for exercise, simple bikes for normal people seem few and far between. We need to accentuate the "average" here. We need to get the average person to start thinking about good, basic bicycles for both exercise and transportation. (Think of it as cross-training!) It's got to be better than a big, bouncy ball.

Health trends come and health trends go. The bicycle has been with us for over 100 years – and it's not going anywhere. If anything, we'll see more bicycles in the years to come . . . but not out of choice. Don't want to look foolish on a bike?

Better start practicing now!

🚲 🚲 🚲

This piece first appeared in Mason's Wire Donkey Bike Zine. *For subscription info, contact Mason St. Clair, Editor and Founder, at masonbike@aol.com.*

THE NEXT THIRTY YEARS? (HOW ABOUT THE NEXT FIFTY?)

By Chip Haynes

Who's to say how long a wise, healthy cyclist can beat the sands of time?
I'm betting on the rider.

My deep, dark secret: I've given up on rock 'n roll. Lately, when I've had to drive the department's van on errands, I've been listening to country music. Contemporary music is just stupid, and the oldies are so, well, old. (And besides, the oldies stations play nothing but commercials for antacids and arthritis medicines.) So I found a country music station, and it's not so bad. It's nice to actually hear the words again.

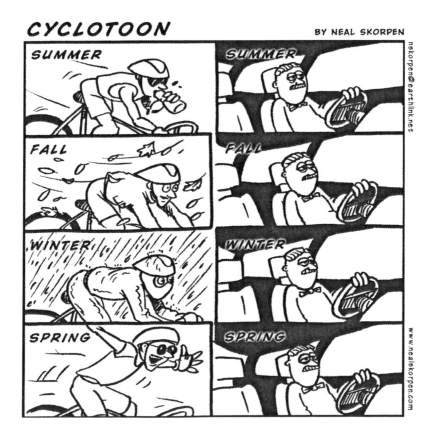

One of the songs I heard the other day was about a guy turning thirty, and all the things he'd decided to do differently for his next thirty years. I can identify, but you'll have to kick it up a notch or two. Make it the next fifty years, and I'm there.

So, what would he change? Oh, it's mostly the usual stuff: Eat more salads, sleep better, drink less bad stuff and more lemonade, you know – that whole health thing. Stuff that you and I probably do everyday, anyway.

Now I'll admit, I was never all that wild. Never smoked, never drank, never could stay up terribly late. So I'm not completely out of bounds. Oh, sure, I stopped riding a bicycle there for about twenty years or so, but I'm back – big time. I got my diet together and I'm putting on more miles and less pounds. Early to bed and early to rise makes a man truly annoying to his coworkers, but what fun!

Bad habits? Not sure I have any. No more ice cream, no more caffeine, no more sodas – and I can't remember my last hamburger. I don't gamble, I keep my language polite, love my wife and pet my dog. I even vote.

So will all of this get me through the next fifty years?

I'd like to see at least 100. I'm partway through my fifties now, and I'm in pretty good shape. Not Lance Armstrong good shape, mind you, but okeydokey good shape. And getting better all the time. Another fifty? Why not? As long as I can keep riding my bicycle!

I think that's the key to it, and it's more than just the exercise I get from pedaling. Sure, it's a good, low-impact workout. Great for the heart, and keeps the legs limber and all, but there's more to it: Bicycling sets you free, both physically and mentally. It keeps you awake, in every sense of the word.

Bicycling lets me get out and see the world, and really feel a part of that world. No glass-and-steel awful-mobile, insulating you from everything. Go for a ride and see, smell, hear and touch the whole world – nothing like a little sensory overload to keep from nodding off! With a little luck, I'll be pedaling for the next fifty years. And as long as I can pedal, I'll have no complaints.

So let's raise a glass of calcium-fortified orange juice and toast the next fifty years. Will I really be riding my bicycle in the year 2057? Who knows? I'm going to give it my best shot, no doubt about it. Here's to great long-range plans – and the health to carry them through! Eat right, get your rest, and ride your bicycle. I think that last one is very important.

Viva le Bicycle, y'all!

🚲 🚲 🚲

This piece first appeared in Mason's Wire Donkey Bike Zine. *For subscription info, contact Mason St. Clair, Editor and Founder, at masonbike@aol.com.*

SHIFTING AHEAD:
PREDICTIONS FOR CYCLING IN THE 21ST CENTURY

Predictions by Richard Fries, Maurice Tierney and Jim Joyce

On the eve of the new millennium, two leaders in cycling journalism and this editor peered into the crystal ball to see what would emerge in the cycling world in the next 100 years. Here's a sampling of what we found (the forecasts about gas prices, commuting, and GPS systems have already come true!)

Richard Fries
(Editor and Founder, *The Ride* and *Bike Culture*)

+ By 2010, gasoline supply will begin to undulate. Prices in the U.S. will top three dollars per gallon, about the same time Transportation Enhancement Act (TEA-21) projects are completed. Sales and usage of bikes for commuting, coupled with mass transit construction, will explode.

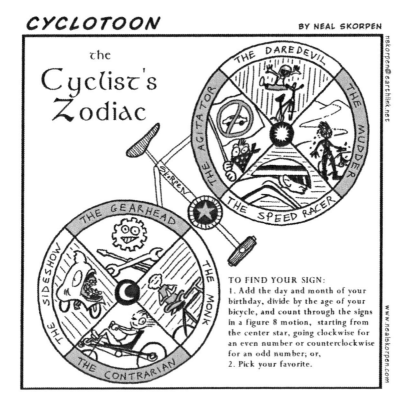

CYCLOTOON BY NEAL SKORPEN

+ By 2015, the National Park Service will completely ban automobiles in parks. The bicycle tourism business will grow accordingly.

+ By 2030, the demand for agricultural land to feed the 12 billion earth residents will be greater than demand for suburban housing on acre lots. Urban real estate will skyrocket in value; urban cycling will continue to grow.

+ By 2050, however, faced with a complete elimination of petroleum reserves, the world will be forced to develop nuclear/solar/wind/coal/trash/anything you can burn fuel sources to run power plants. Attempts to regulate automobile usage, however, could spark a "road warrior" apocalypse with cyclists possibly turning up on the wrong side of the war.

+ Americans will produce several Tour de France champions, thereby giving bike riding the marketing sex appeal that made driving automobiles so popular.

Maurice Tierney
(Publisher, *Dirt Rag*)

I predict we'll burn up all the fossil fuels in our SUVs and start riding bikes everywhere. Then we'll live in a Utopian society where people actually get along with each other. Peace.

Jim Joyce
(Editor and Founder, *The Bicycle Exchange*)

+ All public transit buses will finally be equipped with bike carriers on the front or rear of the bus.

+ More mountain bikers will buy road bikes; more road bikers will buy mountain bikes. Well-rounded cyclists (not well-rounded stomachs) will be the norm.

+ A small, clip-on module with a wireless earphone will harness "Global Positioning Satellites" to give the cyclist an audio cue sheet on how to get just about anywhere.

+ Lifecycles at the local YMCA will be equipped with virtual reality goggles and moveable handlebars. Instead of flipping through a magazine during a workout, riders will plug in whatever race they feel like joining. (You ain't got a chance, Lance!)

+ Despite plenty of worthy attempts by nutrition companies to replace it, the almighty banana will continue to reign as the undisputed World Champion of Cycling Foods.

+ Despite a loss of some customers, most will continue to buy bikes from bike shops for that proverbial "look in the eye" that is absent from e-commerce.

+ Proudly delivering the January, 2021 inaugural address to the citizens of the United States will be none other than: President Lance Armstrong. (What a country!)

CONSIDER THE POSSIBILITIES

WANDERINGS

Be careful going in search of adventure – it's ridiculously easy to find.

—William Least Heat Moon
from *Blue Highways: A Journey Into America*

REMEMBERING HANK

By Jim Joyce

A mentor can emerge anywhere, even on a weeklong bike tour.

Something, somewhere, somehow was jabbing invisible knitting needles into my right knee. The joint hurt. Badly. I was becoming more and more convinced that I'd be walking with a permanent limp when this mistaken venture was all over.

"Hank," I finally said, "It's really killing me."

"Your first tour, right?" Hank said, calmly, not even changing cadence.

"Yeah, but I did do fifty miles a couple of times last week. And the week before, I . . ."

"It'll be all right," Hank said. "Just keep riding . . . it'll go away . . . in a few minutes . . . you'll see."

Ten miles to go. We'd already done sixty-eight into a headwind along flat-as-a-pancake northwestern Ohio farm roads. My shoulders, hands, and wrists just plain ached. But my knee really concerned me. And it was a scorcher of a sunny, August day: The kind of day when road kill smelled so bad you could taste it in your throat. Worse, the weather forecast called for more of the same.

"Uh, okay," I mumbled, thinking Hank was nuts. No, not nuts, but downright evil. For a second I saw red horns and a red tail swinging from his saddle. Get hold of yourself. This ride is ninety percent done. But what if I never ride again? What, quit on the first day of a six-day tour? Ain't gonna happen. . . . I gotta finish this stinkin' ride. Hank must know what he's talking about. But this knee . . .

"It'll go away." Hank added. "You'll work out that kink before long. Just stay with it."

"You really think?"

"Tomorrow, it'll be fine." Hank said. "You'll get stronger each day."

Who's he kidding?

"I'll take your word for it, Hank," I said, wincing. "But this headwind ain't helping!"

He smiled and laughed, having knocked off about seven hours of flat riding in ninety-degree heat.

But that was pure Hank, who became my riding buddy and mentor on that well-run, budget-minded bike tour across Ohio all those years ago. (Hank's real name and the company will not be identified out of respect for his privacy.) I was in the last leg of day one. Ahead of me were five days of touring at an average of seventy-five-plus miles per day. I was a novice long distance rider in my late twenties, sore and worried. Was I out of my element completely? Would I even finish? Would this end up as one embarrassing regret?

Not according to Hank. And he was right . . . about the knee and many other things that week. This fellow twelve years my senior made a positive impact on me. We began the week as perfect strangers in a van heading across Ohio and ended it as genuine friends.

Difference in Age and Wisdom

It seems Hank had left behind many bad habits that I still dabbled in, including staying up late, drinking too much beer, snacking on junk food, and looking for a party. I had no doubt that Hank had experienced his share of wild living. He had a sharp wit and a good sense of humor. He never preached, never wagged his finger. He simply preferred and practiced healthy living.

After a ride I felt like sneaking out for a couple of beers. Hank had a Diet Pepsi. That was his "splurge." While I was hoping to strike up a conversation with a female rider or two in the evening – turned out we were all too exhausted – Hank phoned his wife at 9 P.M. sharp and never missed a night. In the morning, while I was frantically getting my clothes and stuff together for the day, Hank was patiently waiting and giving his bike or mine a quick tune-up. One evening, a group of us strolling through a small town stumbled across an amateur theater company's free rehearsal of "Damn Yankees." Afterward and for the next few days, Hank was heard to belt out a "damn" good rendition of "You Gotta Have Heart," keeping fellow riders smiling.

"All days are good, some are even better," was his daily mantra, one I'd never heard before but have since never forgotten.

We rode . . . we talked. We rode . . . we talked. We downed a lot of water and food. We talked. After a few days of long rides, cyclists touring together learn a lot about one another.

"All days are good, some are even better."

Pasts and Presents

Hank's attitude and outlook were bright, though his life experiences were not always so. I learned he almost dropped out of school, then served in Vietnam. He'd logged one failed marriage and was now discussing the challenges of being a good parent to the daughter of his second wife. Many siblings of his large childhood family no longer kept in touch. He had a little brother who had done time in prison. Hank had a good plant manager job – despite the lack of a college degree – but he never knew if and when his plant would close or if he would be transferred.

"I gotta make it to a 'chew out' session at the plant first thing next Monday," he said, next to the last day of the tour. "Yeah, every once in a while, they give me hell."

His was a high-pressure job, no doubt. And you could tell he wasn't looking forward to Monday. The sleep habits, the good diet, the humor, the routines, the fitness – no wonder he was the plant supervisor. He could hack it. He knew how to live. I wouldn't doubt he was a religious man but he didn't wear it on his sleeve.

Like Hank, I'd experienced my share of ups and downs. Part of my booking this trip was to help put behind me a recently broken relationship and to consider whether to remain in my present job and town. Funny how a good, tough, week-long bike tour can help to sort things out. Maybe it's the cadence and rhythm, or maybe the change of scenery. Most likely, it's all that time – time just to talk and think. It's time that is so scarce in our busy, everyday lives.

Cranking Away

By the time day five arrived, I felt great. I couldn't believe it. Hank was right again. Now I could easily hang with him and my youth began to give me a distinct advantage in climbing and endurance. Our route had become much hillier, similar to my home terrain, and I was pumped. Hank, in turn, lived in a flat state and – though he liked a hill or two – was not pleased with a continuous supply of them.

Early in the morning of day six, our final ride, the staff informed us that the road-marking crew's measurements were fouled. The evening before each ride, the crew had painstakingly marked roads with spray paint arrows and charted the entire itinerary along the state's backroads. Their work had been excellent, but this time they weren't sure because of some unexpected construction and faulty figuring. They said it would be probably be about seventy-five miles.

"All days are good, some are even better," said Hank as we proceeded to gobble down a hearty, filling breakfast.

Seventy-five miles? Ha! It turned out to be ninety grueling, hilly and hot ones. This day witnessed a role reversal of sorts in our partnership. After about sixty miles, Hank hit The Wall – that mythical barrier that tells a rider he or she's just about out of juice. I was worn but feeling good. Hank's head was hanging and he grimaced every time we came around a bend or crested a hill, only to discover another standing right in front of us. And he was looking older to me, maybe not the whole twelve years my senior, but the forehead lines, thinner hair, the bits of gray frosting above the ears – the signs of middle age encroaching – were suddenly more pronounced. More pronounced, too, were a toughness and a vulnerability that I hadn't yet seen in him.

"Damn, there's a lot of hills around here," he said, wiping sweat from his forehead. "Damn!" Hank was only human, a regular guy, and now I finally realized it.

It was hot. Real hot. The mercury climbed toward 100. The sky was clear but the air was dank like a bathroom after a hot shower.

We stopped a few times to rest our legs and drained our water bottles just minutes after refilling them. At a roadside fruit market, we chomped a few oranges for quick fuel and cramp prevention, then saddled up for the final leg of the route. Our town of destination, according to fellow riders at this stand, was somewhere between five and fifteen miles away. No one was certain. We hoped it was more like five.

It was fifteen.

Hank and I were both cussing and moaning as we began to think we'd never see the town where our cars lay idle.

Until . . . yes! We spotted the town's water tower, that triumphant beacon along Ohio roads that signals a town is within spitting distance. Our pace picked up. We looked at each other and shared grins of relief. We high-fived without swerving one inch.

Within minutes, we wheeled from farmland into the outskirts of that neat-and-tidy, proverbial Ohio town. By this time, we were hooting and hollering. We sped into the parking lot and dismounted. I kissed the asphalt. Hank chuckled and shook his head.

"We did it!" he said, "But this last day was hell. Real hell."

We each hit the restroom, splashed our faces, and then grabbed our gear from the company truck. Riders were trickling in. I felt like relaxing and taking my time since I lived only about an hour away. Hank, though, had to drive westward across a couple of states and had to prepare for that Monday "chew out" meeting. He needed to get going.

We exchanged business cards and home addresses, joked a bit and then shook hands heartily. Hank was looking fit as a fiddle and the twinkle was back in his eye. I was glad to have been of help to him that day, encouraging him as he had me days earlier. I felt I'd grown immensely as a biker, and – pardon the cliché – as a person.

He bid farewell and sped off in his small pickup truck.

Epilogue

I never heard from Hank again. I meant to write him promptly, but lost his address in a move of my own. A year or so after the tour I located it and fired off a card. The card was returned, marked "Addressee Has Moved, Forwarding Order Expired." I knew that he would get the same response if he had tried sending me a note.

Seventeen years have passed since that tour. I am seven years older than Hank's very age on the trip. After the tour, I moved once again and, even later, relocated to another city. I am now settled, happily married, and am living a lifestyle much like that of my old riding buddy.

Perhaps his plant closed. Perhaps he was promoted and transferred to another plant. Perhaps he opened a bike shop. Perhaps he's still tuning up neighbor kids' bikes, his favorite hobby.

Hank, whatever you're doing, wherever you are, I'd like to say, "Thank you, my friend." And remember . . .

All days are good, some are even better.

ᚖ ᚖ ᚖ

VERMONT'S FINEST

By Jim Joyce

Mike Gallagher is a unique giant of the Vermont outdoors, widely known as an Olympic cross-country skiing champion in the 1960s and, more recently, as an exceptional guide to the great outdoors. I was fortunate enough to join Mike in the summer of 1998 for a tailored mountain bike ride through Green Mountain National Forest. The adventure began as such . . .

I fear that the rest and relaxation of my honeymoon in Vermont are to be abruptly put on hold as Mike swings his van into the parking lot of The Cortina Inn, near Killington. Meanwhile, I'm stretching hard, knowing my many weeks of nuptial planning have left me physically unfit for any kind of serious mountain biking. But there he is, hopping out of the van and briskly walk-running toward me. His eyes are as sharp a blue as any Irish eyes I've ever seen. He flashes a wide, pearly smile and shakes my hand with a certain grip. He then barely lets go before he is on the roof of the van, pulling off a beautiful new Cannondale mountain bike. All the

IT STILL REQUIRES YOUR FULL ATTENTION. (FOOL)

while, he quizzes me, "Do you need a helmet? . . . What size bike do you need? . . . How tough of a ride do you want to do? . . . How do you like this Cannondale?"

He checks my size on the brand new Cannondale. The fit is perfect. Full suspension. Best darn mountain bike I'd ever sat upon. I'm ready to begin this special morning tour.

"Hey, I appreciate you doing this for me . . . and on such short notice."

"No problem!" Mike shoots back, full of energy at 7 A.M. "Somehow today, though, I've got to scout the river to find some trout for a guy from Montana who I'm fly-fishing with tomorrow."

"You do that, too? Fly fishing?"

"Uh-huh. And do you know how hard it's been to find trout in this heat?"

"Oh?"

"This summer's been so hot and dry they're not even interested in eating," he said, his blue eyes intent even in this sidebar conversation. "Yeah, it'll be tough to find some for him."

A Man of Many Talents

Mike's a mountain biking guide, primarily, but he also takes visitors to his neck of the woods for hunting, fishing and hiking excursions – among other things. Plus, he's a ski guide and instructor during the winter.

Mike's life has been as animated as his personality. His father, who trained with the ski troops in World War II, decided to move the family from New York City to skiing country after the war, when Mike was five.

Mike became such an excellent alpine skier that he medalled for the U.S. Olympic team. He starred in two Olympics during the '60s. He says his love of bicycling began as a method of cross-training for skiing. He was an avid road cyclist, but was bitten early by the mountain biking bug, which he finds "much more interesting." Now his frequent tours keep him in excellent shape – trim, but solid as a rock.

One thing is clear from the beginning: Mike is not just another jock. He's a Vermont "Renaissance man" and – whether we are driving along a farm-and-flower-dotted blue highway or biking a dirt forest road alongside a cascading creek – Mike anxiously provides bits of fact and opinion on a collection of matters. He covers it all:

+ A careful description and criticism of the costly attempts to bring back the native salmon population to the narrow White River. The result has been a sharp decline in native trout.

+ Stopping to point out "deer scratches" in the dirt road, where deer literally scrape the road for salt.

- Admiring a large, perfect vegetable garden bordered by lush wildflowers, and planted by two very elderly friends along the bike route.

- Dismounting so we can measure the size of our hands against the fresh tracks of a Vermont moose.

"See how spread out the toes are? And the distance between the prints?" Mike asks, intently. "You can tell he was trotting, not just walking. He must have heard something and got scared. Maybe us."

Make no mistake, however, this maverick is here to bike and he's not taking it easy on a cream-puff, online magazine editor. Because we only have a few hours, Mike takes me on a test ride of sorts, the one he uses on the first morning of a multi-day group tour. It shows him the varied abilities of the individual bikers and gives him an idea of how challenging to make the next days' trips. Often, the group will be divided into two or three levels and each will get its chance to bike at the best-suited level. Another guide usually accompanies him.

Let the Ride Begin

For this novice-intermediate mountain biker not in prime shape, it is perfect. We park the van at a gravel lot alongside the White River, unload, mount our bikes (his, a blue Specialized Stumpjumper), and ride about two miles along a two-lane highway with very little traffic. Next we turn down a side road and begin our two-mile ascent up a lush, shady, dirt road toward the top of a forest ridge. Music is provided by the constant splashing of Pine Brook, filled with white boulders and marked by frequent, small waterfalls. An excellent place to pitch a tent or stop for a lunch, the canopy of trees and the rush of the cold water keeps the banks cool and comfortable.

The ascent is long and steady, but the rewards during and at the end (the descent!) are well worth it. It is along here that Mike points out the deer scratches, moose tracks, and moose droppings. What a treat for this Western Pennsylvania boy who has seen deer but none of these other rarities. At the end of the road – mainly a logging path at this point – we arrive at the trailhead, which is well-marked with signs reading, "The Pine Brook Trail."

Mountain bike access to this trail and many others, says Mike, is hotly contested and is continuing on a "watch and see" basis. He says mountain bikers have a bad name in some Vermont circles and National Forest authorities are granting them access for a trial evaluation period. Mike is hopeful that mountain bikers turn out in big numbers to use the trails but that they mind their manners and keep the area clean and in perfect shape. He doesn't want them to spoil a good thing. Losing trail access is still a real fear, he says, but he's adamant that mountain biking is a perfect fit for Vermont.

The grade levels and we slowly pedal from the narrow dirt road into the shade of a thick forest of pine and hardwoods. We are at the top of the mountain and there is no turning back. Mike nods toward a steep, skinny trail just ahead.

"Just follow me and you won't have any trouble," he says with a grin. "Oh, and make sure you hold on tight and ride up high off the saddle. And brake when you have to but don't squeeze too hard and too long. You'll lock up and wipe out."

I'm scared, all right, but psyched to reap my reward for the long climb. "I'll be okay," I say, pretending to be confident. "But don't lose me."

"No problem," he assures me. "You'll be fine. This is the best part of the trip . . . Here I go . . ."

Mike launches his bike and begins to fly downhill, through the trees, escaping into the green of the narrow trail.

I hustle to follow. Whoaaa! I'm rushing downhill, holding tight, hopping in and out of dips in the trail, keeping steady, and catching glimpses of Mike's jersey, while small branches graze my helmet and shades. It's rugged and – yes – downright steep. There's just enough clearing to plainly see the dark track. The descent is long – two miles! Mike calls back now and then, reminding me to ride high, not to brake too hard. I'm absorbing the shocks of the bumps and dips, having a blast!

As I near the bottom, I see Mike slowing and dismounting so I ease up, preparing to stop, tickled that I am still upright. A gate straddles the flat area at the bottom of the trail, and feeling a bit cocky about my performance, I attempt to ride slowly around its outer post, as Mike had just done. Whoops! Like a rookie, and in full view of my guide, I wipe out on the easiest part of the course. Oh, well, I need a little dirt to show my wife. Mike gets a good laugh, too.

The end of the trail dumps us right back onto the lower portion of the dirt road we ascended earlier. We coast pleasantly down the road alongside Pine Brook and make it back to the paved blue highway that leads us back to the van. . . .

His Day's Just Starting

. . . It's almost noon as Mike drops me back at the Cortina. Me? I get to go eat like a horse, rest, and enjoy the rest of my fine Vermont honeymoon. Mike? . . . "This afternoon, I have to go find those trout spots," he says. "Tonight, my boy [one of two] and I will probably head out for a few hours of singletrack after supper. We like to get a good ride in together on my days off."

Whew! Gets me tired just thinking about this human dynamo. Thanks, Mike, for the inspiration, the perspiration, and the terrific experience of rubbing shoulders with "Vermont's Finest."

⚲ ⚲ ⚲

CALIFORNIA ANGEL

By Bill Joyce

*Unexpected blessings are the best kind, as a teacher finds out along Highway 1,
south of the San Francisco Bay, on New Year's Eve.*

Biking down the coast, I'm cruising with a tailwind, the royal blue Pacific to my right, all good things on my mind – and I pop two flats.

A fellow biker helps me with one; I fix the other. Ten more miles and my rear tire's flat, cooked, kaput.

It's 5 P.M., gorgeous coastal sunset, full moon, and I'm stuck twenty-five miles from Santa Cruz (en route to visit an old Peace Corps mate and reinforcing a New Year's resolution to ride more frequently). The rear tire's shot; no way to find the hole on the already thrice-patched tube. I'm dead meat.

I walk down Highway 1, thumb out; I'll take either direction. I come to a call box – the cop says hang tight for an hour. No, he says, AAA won't respond to a biker's call even if you have AAA. I continue to thumb in both directions. Now it's 5:15, already dark, and my friend, Mike, is waiting. We planned to head to a club called Palookaville, to see his kid play in his group, named the Haskells – yup, after Eddie – at 6:45, part of a First Night concert.

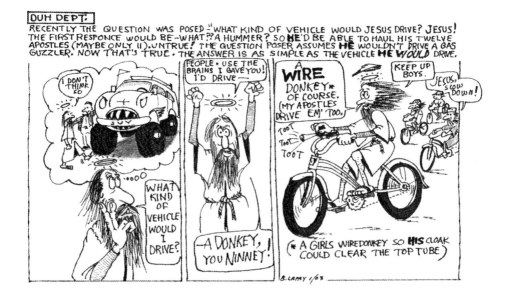

I've pulled out my Levi's and street shoes. I hope the cop shows up in an hour and gives me a ride, somewhere, I don't care where.

Ten minutes later, a truck with a camper shell pulls over. I jog down the dark road, bike at my side. Tom from San Francisco is going to Santa Cruz. I cop the ride.

I'm ga-ga. He's maybe twenty-five, but his vibe is the best of the '60s. He turns down the Gregorian chant on his cassette. He's got a display across his dashboard – some green organic stuff. He says he started this drive reflecting on the year, wishing that he'd done more to help people out. Suddenly, I appear on the roadside, all the better that I have a bike – he bikes, too. He's off to spend New Year's with friends. They'll reflect on regrets and thankfuls for the past year, and what they can accept for the next one.

We drive the twenty-five miles to Santa Cruz. He lets me off a half block from my friend's house. I arrive in time to bathe, change, and head off to Palookaville just in time.

Of course, here I am stuck an extra day. Santa Cruz, Mountain Bike Capital of California, has no bike shops open on the New Year's holiday. I need a presta-valved tube, probably two, and a new tire. So I hang out with Mike, and drink in the pleasures of the New Year. Bike shop's to open January 2. I'll get what I need, catch a twenty-mile ride by bus up the coast, and pedal the final thirty miles to Half Moon Bay where I parked my car . . .

This guy, Tom from San Francisco – young, long-haired, spirit-filled, looking at New Year's the way you're supposed to (Janus: Roman god, two heads, one forward, one back – looking ahead; looking behind). Me, the impulsive long distance biker, the receiver of this angel's lift.

🚲 🚲 🚲

DESERT STORM

By John Stuart Clark

In this adaptation from his book, After the Gold Rush, *Scotsman John Stuart Clark experiences the full force of nature while crossing America along the line of the Gold Rush.*

At the risk of stating the obvious, cyclists are a vulnerable species. At best, our defenses are flimsy – strips of plastic, Gore-Tex wraps, and a pudding basin of expanded polystyrene. Against the elemental forces of nature, they provide scant protection but, for the strong at heart, it is the very susceptibility of the cyclist that makes rolling through a landscape such a rewarding experience. Now and again, however, Mother Nature slings something at us which is over the top.

Take a short ride I recently endured down a straight road in the middle of Wyoming. The action takes place over fifteen miles, maximum, in a barren landscape all had deserted except the Big Yin and a few dumb critters. In the distance were the broken backbones of the Rockies, rearing up like dinosaurs emerging from a sea of sagebrush desert. On either side of me, the terrain barely undulated, but Pacific Creek had carved a meandering course that left an occasional head-high bluff exposed. That was it as far as features and shelter were concerned, unless you consider fence posts and a rare road sign any kind of protection against driving wind and rain or a vicious sun.

In theory, I was well removed from America's Tornado Alley, where twisters perennially wreak havoc across the prairies, but this year the weather was proving ever more fickle. It was a month on from an Oklahoma disaster, where the tornado reached an unprecedented F6 on the Fujita scale (inconceivable). Twisters had been spinning strong and wild in sheltered states like Wyoming, not renown for this sort of meteorological mayhem, and it had been an unusually wet start to the summer.

As I rode through a sweltering day, I watched cumulus clouds build on the horizon and slowly congregate into small grey thunderheads. The ever-present westerly picked up pace and cranked the thermostat up a whole lot of notches. Over a period of half an hour, the thunderheads grew exponentially, piling on the layers of black and bilious pitch. Across their tops, over twenty miles up, dull lights morphed through a restricted spectrum like failing disco lights. Similar to weak auroras, these were the signatures of sprites. I knew enough meteorology to be more than a little concerned. Sprites are a sign that an esoscale convective complex is approaching or, in plain English, one mother of a storm.

Things began moving fast. By late morning, storm front and cyclist met. Except for my grinding crank and the low wuthering of the escalating wind, the landscape fell silent. Over my head, the elements began acting out a drama as powerful as any Shakespearean tragedy.

To the north were ranged the forces of good – a deep blue sky lined with battalions of white clouds. To the south, beneath the mass of dark forces, the horizon blazed as one fusillade of sheet lightning after another exploded from the barrels of heaven's howitzers.

The rumble of hooves was the rumble of thunder sweeping across the plateau with increasing volume and speed. I upped my cadence to pedal out of the battle zone, aiming for a thin wedge of blue that opened in the ranks of the enemy. For a moment, I thought I had ridden clear. An almighty explosion banged into my eardrums, deafening me. A second later, a jagged shaft of megavolts thumped into the ground maybe a mile away. Beneath the swirling charge of hell's dark knights, lightning zipped across the firmament. More forks grounded, landing closer. I was the tallest element in the landscape and a sitting target.

The first wave passed overhead with only a splattering of rain. I was already wearing my waterproof jacket, leaving off the trousers so my legs could pump like fury unimpeded. Before I knew what had hit me, the second wave charged in, accompanied by a ferocious wind that stopped me dead and splattered me with sand. I ground forward again, leaning into the storm.

Without the warning of thunder, a blinding flash of lightning shot out of the clouds and thudded into the desert across the road from me. It sounded like fireworks – a demented squib, magnified and out of control. In the course of a split second, the earth shook, my ears popped, the wind was whacked out of my lungs and my head felt as if a hot metal wire had been banged through my left temple and yanked out the right. I swerved uncontrollably across the road and came to a clumsy halt. Where the lightning had struck, a cloud of steam lingered. I felt stunned.

Opening a sluice gate, the heavens rained down hail stones the size of gob-stoppers. I dumped the bike and assumed a crouched position beside the road, holding my hands over my head to fend off the onslaught. There was nowhere to hide. The best I could do was tuck myself into a ball and let my hands and back take the full force of the frozen grape shot. Close behind me, I heard another squib plunge to earth. The impact lifted me off my feet and threw me forwards. With bum higher than head, I knelt in a field of white gob stoppers recovering from another hot wire lobotomy. It started to bucket down.

"Yo! Get in!"

The shout came from the wound-down window of a car that had pulled up on the opposite side of the road. A woman was beckoning me to get out of the torrential rainfall. I obviously wasn't thinking straight.

"I'm going the other way," I screamed. "Thanks."

I wasn't going anywhere and the moment she pulled away, I had regrets.

Returned to my senses and aware I was saturated, there was only one course of action. Uprighting my bike, I leapt on the saddle and pedaled away as fast as the wind and zapped muscles would allow. My body temperature had plummeted. I had to light a fire in myself, fast, and the only way to stoke a blaze in these conditions was the frantic pounding of legs.

Along a washed out line, I carved through a freezing monsoon, floodwaters streaming down my body underneath my clothing. I couldn't see a hand in front of my face. After a quarter hour of trying to outrun hypothermia, the rain fizzled out, the dark forces parted, and the sun shone through. I started to steam.

On reflection, it had been a terrifying experience. When my frontal lobe wasn't frying, my brain worked double-time, rattling through options, survival scenarios and vague memories of what to do and where to be in a lightning storm. Probably the reason my brain was frantically scrolling was because I was shitting bricks at the other end. I had totally forgotten what to do and where to be in a lightning storm.

Five miles further on, my bottom lip quivering with cold, I climbed a low hill. From the top, I saw the village of Farson in the distance, bathed in a warm glow that transformed the grey desert into green prairie. It was a crossroads community and river crossing, and had to have a cafe. Between rows of trashy trailer homes, junk-strangled bungalows and one ugly geodesic hovel, I shivered up to the crossroads.

In the Oregon Trail Cafe, a cowboy said, "You that bicyclist rode through the storm? Man, you gotta be crazy as a coyote under a full moon. I overtook you an' offered a lift. Guess ya didn't hear me."

I didn't even see him and his beat up pick-up drive past.

Outside the window, steam rose from the flooded car park. The sky cleared and warm rays lit up the bridge straddling the Big Sandy River. About 150 years ago, pioneers, Mormons, and gold seekers traveling west to promised lands forded the river at Farson, then probably no more than a tented trading post. According to their diaries, they too encountered storms like nothing they had experienced in Europe. Unlike myself, they had the shelter of their Conestoga wagons.

I tore into a homemade burger the size of a hubcap, optimistic that the remains of the day would be warm and bright now the heavens had off-loaded their pent up rage. What I failed to see through the cafe windows was another storm system building in the southwest. I stepped out into a humid oven and instantly flooded with perspiration. In front of me, due west and the direction I was headed, the sky was a deep ultramarine. Ten degrees south it was black as night. I started out again, thinking I might be able to outride and dodge the next storm.

Less than a mile from the river crossing, I was hit by another rush of warm wind. Knowing what came next, I thought to turn back. In the field beside me, a farmer continued to plough a furrow, seemingly unperturbed by the weather closing in. Maybe this attack wouldn't be as bad? I slipped on waterproof leggings, and continued cycling, keeping an eye out for a storm drain I might dive in. Once again, white light strobed on the horizon and fork lightning darted from beneath the glutinous clouds. I looked to my right. The farmer was beating a retreat for home. With a clap of thunder, the tractor disappeared behind a veil of gob-stoppers. They fell at an acute angle, driven by the gale, and this time were no bigger than marbles.

In quick succession, the monsoon followed the hailstorm. I tried curling my body into a drainage ditch less than two feet deep, hoping the levee might provide some protection. It did, until a trickle of runoff grew into a mini tidal wave boring down the ditch. Relieved that rapid-fire lightning had kept its distance, grounding several hundred yards away, I remounted and rode into the storm. The lashing I received was freezing and ferocious. The road disappeared under spray and water, its course marked by hovering snow poles, their bottom three-foot line invisible.

Ten minutes that felt like an hour later, the rain stopped and a shaft of sunlight struggled through. Behind the crack in the grey ceiling, another front was moving in, and another behind that. The landscape was flat as a pancake with nothing remotely approaching a ranch house standing tall. I was in for a cold, wet and miserable night under canvas. If I had any hope of waking the next morning without a raging temperature and double pneumonia, I had to stoke a glow if not a blaze in my whole body, not just my legs.

In a dry gulch known as Simpson's Hollow, I brought the day to an early conclusion, hunkering down for the next onslaught. Uncontrollable shivers impeded rapid erection of the tent. Low spirits and mental panic had me making basic mistakes as I fumbled through a process I could normally do in my sleep. Finally I crawled into the sleeping bag, loaded it with every item of clothing I carried and rubbed myself to a dull glow.

The expected torrential downpour never happened. Cautiously, I crawled out at twilight and found myself under a crystal clear sky. A lone antelope stood on a low bluff twenty meters from me and stamped her hoof, angry at my cramping her roaming of the open range. In the sagebrush, spiders were already at work mending their shredded webs.

I took a stroll down to the Big Sandy for a strip wash. The dust devil had penetrated orifices I never knew I had. When I removed my clothing, I saw my skin was blotchy with bruises. I had taken a pummeling under the hail, but it was a small price to pay for the raw and exhilarating experience of riding through an unbridled onslaught of elemental nature. I'm not a religious person, but I had witnessed such overwhelming forces and scales of movement that something eternal had to be at work. After such a day, one can only pause and wonder.

᚛ᚋ ᚛ᚋ ᚛ᚋ

Adapted from After the Gold Rush: A Bicycle Journey Through American History *by John Stuart Clark, available in USA from AK Press (akpress@akpress.org).*

Saharan Margins

By John Stuart Clark

Not content to rest after a thrilling journey across an American desert,
this wandering Scotsman explores the Mother of All Deserts.
That's "Trés courageux," all right!

Friends were impressed, sort of. When they asked what my wife and I were doing for Christmas, instead of the traditional "My parents' place" and a groan, they got a smile and "We're off to the Sahara."

"What, on one of those four-wheel drive safaris?"

"Nope. On bikes."

As jaws thudded to the ground, we reassured them that we were not "transnavigating" the great emptiness. Just going for a nosy, round one corner of it, curious to see, smell and hear what the mother of all deserts is like. (Sahara is a derivation of the Arabic word *sahra*, meaning desert.)

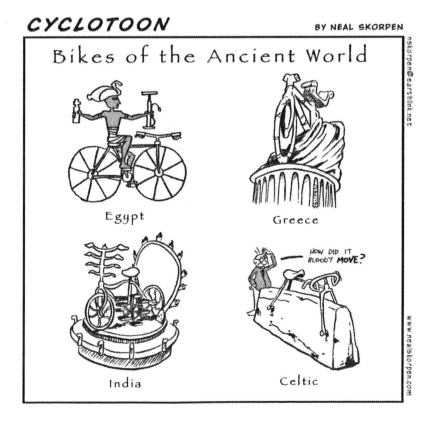

It was about then they recommended counseling. I agreed; sand dunes are stubbornly resistant to the forward motion of thin tires powered by human muscle. It is also true that most pedalers across the Sahara belong to expeditions undertaken by extremely together or extremely reckless cycle explorers, neither of which was an appropriate description for our sedate approach to traveling. We bluffed it out, conscious we were riding into the unknown, confident we would do nothing stupid, satisfied we had prepared ourselves for a hairy time.

Unrest in Algeria ruled out entry into the largest slab of the Sahara in North Africa. We had enough to contend with without bringing politics into the equation, so Libya and Egypt also fell by the way. Reaching the Moroccan desert involves first crossing the Atlas Mountains. States south of the 25th parallel required all sorts of visas and jabs that we hadn't the time or money to obtain. Tunisia, however, offered cheap flights, easy access to the Grand Erg Occidental (one of the vast seas of sand dunes) and the Chott El Djerid, a large salt lake bordered with palmeries and oases, dry for at least ten months of the year. In the fourteenth century, when caravans first poured into this seldom-traveled area, this sink swallowed up thousands of camels and their attendants who strayed from the trail marked with palm stumps. We didn't wish to join them, but to experience such a forbidding place was a must.

Tunisia is also possibly the friendliest country in the Arab world, an important factor when crossing an alien landscape following off-road (*piste*) routes that feature on your map and nobody else's. A rapid scan of discrepancies between cartographic publishers at London's best map shop indicated local help was going to be necessary for steering well clear of the thin salt crust of the chott.

From the Mediterranean coast to the desert is a steady slog in winter. Warm south westerlies skim across the Sahara, gently squeezing between the Jabel Tebaga and the foothills of the Dorsale mountains. They are unstinting, grow stronger in the afternoon, then die as you crawl into your sleeping bag. Under wheel, the tarmac was coarse, but okay when it was there. When it more often wasn't present, passing putt-putts – two-stroke scooters – kicked up enough dust to transform us into a couple of powder puff drag queens, but it was a ride worth tackling.

A night train could easily whisk you blind into Gafsa, the gateway to the desert, but we chose to pedal. It wasn't because of the weather, which during a winter's day ranges between a warm British spring and a hot summer. And it wasn't the money, the culture, the food, or the languages (French and Arabic). It was simply the desire to travel towards the desert, to see its margins and discover how the arid wilderness of sand dunes emerges from the dry fertile farming country of the coastal plain – how the Mediterranean mutates into the African.

On the map there were just six communities between Sfax on the coast and Gafsa, a distance of 169 kilometers. On the ground there were that many in the first 25 km – small farming settlements, the grandest encompassing little more than a mosque, café, store and a handful of breeze block homes, all whitewashed. As we rode west, the distance separating villages grew in proportion to the amount of dust whipped up by the ubiquitous putt-putts. Between each, parade grounds of olive groves disappeared over the horizon, the gap between ranks of gnarled trees growing at an equivalent rate. Land was becoming poor and cheap the closer we got to the desert. By the time we creaked into Gafsa, we were traveling through scrub – slim pickings for the few flocks of lop-eared sheep, which were now the sole indicators of land use. Signs of human habitation had whittled down to a rare adobe dwelling seen through binoculars, with maybe a donkey enclosure woven from olive tree prunings and palm fronds. Now and again, out of nowhere, a child appeared beside the road to gape, or a snarling dog gave chase before being zapped by my Dog Dazzler.

Aside from sand, sky and space, the only elements of nature that seemed to increase in the transition from dry to parched landscapes were the birds. The desolate borders of the Sahara are home to a baffling variety of larks and wheatears, most noticeably the crested larks that hopped onto the road to check us out, ran in front for a few seconds, then flew off for a snack. Holes in the veld (African grassland) no doubt led to the Shangri-Las for gerbils, lizards and desert rats, but we saw none of them. A skulking prairie fox gave us a wide berth one evening, and left its calling card during the night. Except for those encapsulated in key chains at souvenir grottoes, we encountered no scorpions, spiders, mosquitoes or snakes. Had it not been for the herd of camels we spied in the distance, grazing in the flood plain of the Oued El Melah, we could have been crossing a Spanish plain. In our first night of wild camping in the desert it even had the audacity to rain.

Twenty miles on from where the desert officially started, we were beginning to think the white sands that graced so many tourist posters were somewhere way down south. Suddenly the road plunged through less than a hundred meters. From the crest it ran straight as an arrow into the heat haze of infinity. Far off, tufts of stubble were the crownings of date palms and the oasis where the first shower in a week awaited us. Beyond, where earth and sky writhed together in the shimmering haze, we could only guess at what we were heading into. A car pulled over and an Arab teacher of French handed us a bottle of orange juice. "Trés courageux," he kept repeating, as we pointed to our goal, "Trés courageux."

So far the journey had been plain sailing, certainly the cycling. Yes, we had been hassled by kids throwing stones, but we expected some degree of animosity in the wake of the invasion of Iraq, a fellow Arab country. We had suffered the odd run-in with a drunk, and slept communally with a peasant family whose head had wandering hands, which scorched him when I changed places with my wife in the middle of the night. And we had naively followed a beckoning local into the darkest recesses of the Gafsa medina, our paranoia increasing with every darkening bend, only to discover he simply wanted to show us his collection of postcards around the world. He fed us and introduced us to the four generations of his family living in the courtyard shack, and all he asked in return was a postcard from us when we returned home. The vast majority of Arabs were unreasonably friendly and generous in their poverty. When every other vehicle pips a *Ma'assalama* (go in peace), when folks never tire of waving and shouting *Bonsoir* before midday, it was hard to feel anything other than at ease in this country.

The Tunisians are not used to free-range travelers, particularly cyclists. They can't imagine why anybody wouldn't want to be driven from one touristique zone to another in convoys of white 4x4s. We were dogged by their dust clouds for much of our sojourn in the desert, and discovered we had become a sight of special scientific interest to package trippers who really thought we were out on a limb. At a sign pointing to water (which wasn't there), I posed for the camera with up-turned bidons. A screech of brakes followed by billowing dust, and a gaggle of blotchy Germans were seen rooting through their white charger for bottles of mineral water. We were fine, we explained, but thank you. In fact we were barely ten minutes from a village, a troglodyte village where the locals still live underground, that the tourists had totally missed.

The oases of Tozeur and Nefta are both sizeable communities and far from the stereotype of three date palms and a Berber tent pitched beside a puddle. Once important camel train towns, they now traded in tourism, of the pushy variety their Mediterranean countrymen practice. Maybe their history and the vicissitudes of the surrounding desert have made residents more appreciative of the natural phenomena they freely share with travelers. Set in a depression thick with palms and rimmed by Sunni mosques, Nefta's oasis is particularly enigmatic and a magnet for local lads out to impress burka-clad lasses with their swimming prowess. But it is the great chott the two towns reside beside that deflects the independent traveler's attention. Like a big damp depression in an endless Malibu beach, the evaporated salt lake extends to a horizon that belies the earth's curvature.

We rode over it on an asphalt causeway laid by the army back in the 1970s, seventy-eight kilometers of seminal cycling which the convoys rattled off in half an hour, never tasting the salt in the air or testing the silvery quicksand. On an island midway across we ran into Brazilian Luiz Simoes, one of cycling's most respected wilderness riders, and joined his party of three compadres for a few days. They weren't the first foreign cyclists we had encountered. We caught sight of a German in Tozeur on a loaded tandem with a six-year-old "stoker" using kiddie-cranks and his teenaged daughter riding solo. Then there were three Italians in gaudy Lycra we saw coming from 250 kms away, and an English couple dressed like they were nipping down the pub. But that was all.

Kebili is where drivers and motorcyclists aspiring to the Paris-Dakar Rally set out from on practice circuits, but our route into the dunes was anybody's guess.

Cross-referencing maps with the Brazilians, there were three possibilities, all pistes, none likely to be marked. We were heading into the ergs of the Occidental, beyond the oases, where the only vegetation is rows of palm fronds pushed into the ridges of dunes to prevent windblown sand from obliterating the track. We discovered that sand as fine as salt is not deterred by lines of dead leaves. It found its way into everything. To lubricate a bike with anything other than wax would have been folly. And to expect it wouldn't find a way to wipe out the frail piste we opted for was wishful thinking. Ten kilometers beyond the eerie buttes of Blidet it had overwhelmed an entire village, the jumble of flat roofs peaking out of the desert like recumbent headstones.

Though nobody said as much, it was reassuring to have teamed up with Luiz for the crossing. He is of the extremely together variety of adventurer, having pedaled parts of the Sahara where watering holes are more than 400 kms apart. Out here we only needed three consecutive days' supply, but clearly he wallowed in the beauty of this corner of Africa's vast emptiness as much as the novices did. Without him, some might have turned back where the first dunes buried the piste. There is no riding through this stuff, no matter how fat your tires are, but Luiz pushed on, experience telling him that somewhere on the other side the firm track continued. Compass skills were essential (which the Brazilians relied on the British for) and binoculars useful to navigate us through the featureless wasteland. The northeastern Sahara is subtle and baffling, with few landmarks and none that appear on any map. In a tight corner, a wandering Berber is definitely Mohammed-sent.

Ours arrived the night we celebrated my wife's birthday. We had become a little lost, nothing desperate, but sufficient to agree we should call it a day and reconsider our position in the clear light of morning. One of our company had managed to bake a cake (in the desert, on a Trangia stove!) and our circle sat 'round a camel dung fire enjoying the luxury when the nomad emerged out of the night. It was Ramadan and well after dusk, but he said he'd keep our sticky offering for the following night, wrapping his slice in a scarf and tucking it into his shoulder bag. When we asked about our position, he looked aloft. It was a cold clear night and the silence was creepy, but the stars were a canopy of twinkling lights. With total surety he pointed in the direction we needed for rejoining the piste. "So much for GPS," somebody muttered as our friend looked up at the stars and disappeared northwest back into the night.

For those of us from temperate climes, traveling through such an extraordinary environment can be a mystical experience. It is a disarming vacuum, seemingly benign and very romantic, but day and night, summer or winter, the Sahara is potentially lethal. Oscillating between brain frazzling and sub-zero temperatures, it is necessary to carry clothing and sleeping bags for four seasons. Add water and food, and you are riding a reluctant packhorse unhappy with its slippery footing. It is the type of cycling that requires constant vigilance and continual adjustments, but the rewards are much greater than simply a safe passage. In the southwest corner of Tunisia, the Sahara does not demand that you load up your steed with camping gear. On many routes, hotel accommodation is rarely further than a day away, but until you have pedaled deep into the cauldron and slept amongst the dunes, the buttes, the Berber flocks, you haven't begun to experience the full drama of the desert. This place might carry a health warning, but the only way to make sense of the intimidating landscape and extreme climate is to immerse yourself in it.

On our way out of the desert, leaving Africa for the Mediterranean, we did the usual tourist things. Now separated from the Brazilians, we ticked off the camel ride and village souks, visited the locations where George Lucas filmed *Star Wars*, and dug down for sand roses. None were a patch on the ride across the chott or our first contact of the Grand Erg Occidental, when we ditched our bikes and ran off to play in the dunes like kids at the seaside. Time, sand and the Algerian border prevented us from exploring deeper into the wilderness, but as an introduction to African desert riding, this highly accessible bulge of the Sahara must be hard to beat.

It had taken a toll of our machines however. If the pistes were just annoyingly rippled and the sand dunes quite literally a drag, the rocky margins hammered our bikes, particularly the dry river beds my wife and I exploited to steer our way back to civilization. For maybe a couple of weeks in the rainy season the rivers flow. For the rest of the year they provide access for the troglodyte families who live in the riverbanks and clearly own donkeys, not bicycles. By the time we limped back into Sfax, I had long run out of spare spokes and was riding a machine with a serious drink problem.

In the meantime I discovered that African bike shops (think primitive hole in a wall rather than 21st century showroom) have all the spare parts you could wish for, but none of the tools. Apparently the likes of Shimano won't release them for fear the enterprising Africans will start producing cheap replicas. Sat cross-legged on the street, the mechanic used a lump hammer to remove my rear block, striking it with precise but terrifying blows. "Is no problem, mister," his apprentice tried to reassure me as each blow ploughed another furrow deep in my brow. In the meantime, my wife had colonized a corner of the railway station so we could work on the bikes when I returned from the shop. I arrived with all the parts and my block removed, but the rear hub looked decidedly distorted.

As I worked feverishly against the deadline set by the train we needed to catch, the railway staff plied us with strong Arab coffees and sweet Tunisian cakes. It was Ramadan, but we were travelers in need and no prophet is more prescriptive about caring for vulnerable travelers than the nomad Mohammed. When the booking clerk returned to reopen the kiosk, he presented me with a clean cloth and a tub of Swarfega degreaser brought from home. When the train arrived and I was still struggling to true two wheels, he got the conductors to make space in the caboose for me to complete the job en route to Monastir, our point of departure from Tunisia. I couldn't imagine such generosity and assistance being offered in any of the rich western countries I've explored.

Wheeling our wobbly and sand caked machines into the Monastir airport, a security guard became curious about what we had done and where we had been. Though it was his country, he was as impressed by our adventure as our friends back home. "Trés courageux," he said (it was becoming a mantra) as he planted kisses on both our cheeks. Courageous? I think not. Riding away from London's Heathrow airport into the insanity of a British rush hour – now that takes courage.

᚛ ᚛ ᚛

The Anthropology Of Fanaticism: A multicultural study of wheel-lovers at Amstel Gold

By Ella Lawrence

European road races host the wildest and most dedicated of racing fans.
The author embedded herself in the crowd to study the throngs
of fanatics at the Netherlands' Amstel Gold Race.

E very European grows up with cycling. Each year, as the Spring Classics speed through small towns in small countries, kids, families, and revelers take a small step away from their daily routines to cheer on local heroes. Maastricht, the site of the Amstel Gold Race, sits in the Dutch province of Limburgh, tightly straddled by Belgium and Germany. It's a good place to study different fans from different countries.

At 9:30 A.M., before the start, the busiest place in Maastricht's Markt Square is the space surrounding the team buses, which are parked like giant caterpillars. The one with the most action is the CSC bus, probably because all of its riders

are still inside. Their shiny black and red Cervelos are lined up in a perfect row on the side of the bus, and Danish families with small flags affixed to their backpacks wait for a chance to get baseball caps autographed. Old men in wool jerseys on steel bikes with downtube shifters stand toward the back of the crowd, gossiping amongst themselves about past races and today's possible winner (Michael Boogerd of Rabobank is the favorite). While they are interested in the shiny bikes and the gleaming, muscular racers, they've seen it all before and would rather rehash their own glory days.

The riders emerge, and the Danish fans cheer, pumping up their boys for the start. A couple of American students have pushed their way to the front of the group and are excitedly snapping photos of the pros up close.

One fan quips excitedly, "I came to the Netherlands to study partly because I wanted to see some real races. Racing in America is so different. You could never get close to the buses or the racers like this! Security has everything roped off so tightly. Here, the fans are an integrated part of the race."

Pro races on America's west coast, like the San Francisco Grand Prix or the Sea Otter Classic, where vendors and yuppies converge to sip Starbucks lattes and buy next year's fastest wheelset, are a far cry from the Amstel Gold Race scene. Here in the Netherlands, cycling is about camaraderie and competition.

At the start line, the younger fans are excited, chattering amongst themselves and jumping up to catch a glimpse of riders behind the lead motorcycles. The older fans, mostly Dutch men, sit staidly drinking their beers at 10 A.M., sagely contemplating the scene from terrace cafes. By now, everything is accompanied by the inevitable corny techno music that is a cross-cultural phenomenon at any bike race, blaring through speakers mounted on trees to pump up the fans for their favorite riders.

French fans converge, wearing expensive Rudy Projects and smoking cigarettes, talking importantly about relevant race tactics. The Dutch are the most prominent group today, of course, although most Dutch fans readily cede that Belgian fans are the wildest by far.

"They're definitely the craziest cycling fans," admits a Dutch fellow in a Rabobank cycling cap. "All of their TV stations cover the races live, they've got these giant flags all the time, they just go nuts. You should see them when the race is in Belgium!"

A not-so-wild Belgian family occupies a spot on a low wall underneath their giant flag. They're picnicking, bringing their kids up in a true Belgian tradition – at a bike race. A Dutch cameraman scratches his head perplexedly and says that the Belgians, and their flags, have been at the finish line since 8:30 this morning. Indeed, the best spots in front of the big-screen TV suspended from an ancient stone bridge are occupied by Flemish groups clustered under their yellow flag with its black lion. They loudly cheer on their darlings, quaffing beer – the best in the world – brought from home.

Dutch spectators are growing more jovial by the minute, as the cardboard trays of Amstel 'fluitjes' (little flues of beer) are carried out by the dozen. Groups of younger fans in orange T-shirts fight for the camera's attention, singing sentimental nationalistic songs at the top of their lungs.

The stacks of empty plastic cups on terrace tables grow higher as the cheering and singing grow louder, still a full half hour before the racers are to climb to Valkenburg, about ten miles east of Maastricht. The crowd becomes more excited as the announcer's tone picks up. The riders will be by in a mere ten minutes and the crowd can feel their proximity. A T-Mobile support car speeds by, flinging pink inflatable hands to the crowd, as the tiny local speed limit recorder blinks "You are driving too fast." The motorcycles with their flashing lights arrive, and two riders follow them up the mountain, eight minutes off the front. Everyone cheers politely, but what the crowd really wants is the peloton. As the blur of color passes inches in front of their noses, the fans go wild, screaming for their favorites, their countrymen. When the excitement is over, two minutes later, the fans get back to the serious business of drinking.

The race would not pass through Valkenburg again for another two hours, at the finish. While some fans followed the race in their cars, most of the action stayed in Valkenburg, where the taverns and terraces filled up rapidly with groups of fans shouting at televisions that were showing the race in every smoky corner. On an open terrace, a group of German-speaking Belgians kindly shared the stacks of ponchos they'd collected from yet another vehicle (this time a race sponsor) passing out free promotional gifts. Drops started to come down wildly out of clear blue sky, holding true to the unpredictable Netherlands weather patterns.

The crowd at the finish line is smaller than the crowds at the pubs, who prefer to watch the finish on the screens. Only the die-hard cyclist fans are left, mostly Dutch and Belgians. I, however, push my way to the barriers just in time to see the two riders off the front as they pass the 200-meter line. I'm close enough to see the sweat dripping off Boogerd's face as he bites his tongue, probably regretting his early attack as Rebellin pulls around him at the 100-meter line to take the win.

The fans quickly dissemble their makeshift camps and head back to their cars. This race is, after all, just a normal course of a European spring. Riding a clunky borrowed Dutch cruiser back to Maastricht, I made better time than the Fassa Bortolo bus, which trundled along the street, a few feet from my side. The still-Spandexed riders inside looked tired, sweaty, and most of all, human. The glory and the heroism have faded, and they will go home to rest and prepare for tomorrow's workday, just like their fans.

⚨ ⚨ ⚨

Magic (Re)visited At Woodstock

By Alan Ira Fleischmann

An author-cyclist ponders an event that made an indelible impression on the world, not so long ago, and recalls his own trip to Yasgur's Farm years later, via a great bike tour.

Once upon a time, in a little hamlet in upstate New York, a million people crashed a party. Although this party was only supposed to have a couple of hundred thousand people, you know how parties sometimes get out of hand. Somebody tells somebody who tells somebody who tells somebody else, and pretty soon the whole neighborhood shows up. Eventually, the parents totally lose control of the party, which soon becomes a monster. The inadequate supply of munchies is quickly devoured, the septic backs up, and it seems like every junkie

in the world is there, but the music is great. After the smoke clears, everyone looks back on the party and realizes that it was the best!

This was August of the year of *Easy Rider, Butch Cassidy and the Sundance Kid, True Grit, Midnight Cowboy,* and *Oh, Calcutta!* Charles Manson (and his "family") had killed Sharon Tate. Sesame Street wouldn't air until November, *Penthouse Magazine* would not begin publication for another two months, and the New York Mets had not yet won the World Series. What a year it was! Woodstock, however, will probably be remembered as perhaps the single most amazing phenomenon of 1969.

The success of the Woodstock Music Festival, or simply "Woodstock," as it became known, was the unintentional and coincidental result of under-planning, underestimating, bad weather, and Murphy's Law, on a mega-scale. Such musical legends as Jimi Hendrix, Jefferson Airplane, Arlo Guthrie, Joan Baez, The Who, The Grateful Dead, and Santana, to name a few, played host to the largest concert audience ever assembled. Even the lack of food, toilets, medical facilities, and sunshine (it rained the entire weekend) could not dampen the festivities. In spite of all of these shortcomings and the presence of the largest concentration of booze and controlled substances this side of Anheuser-Busch and Warner-Lambert, there were no deaths, and three births. A true twentieth century miracle!

I'm old. I remember Woodstock. I wasn't actually there, but I do remember the 60's, the good times and the bad. I still don't like Hendrix or rain. I get hungry after an hour. I don't do drugs. But looking back with 20/20 hindsight, I would now willingly give the left side from the pair of one of my most important pieces of anatomy to have experienced that brief moment of historical magic, first hand.

When I received a "psychedelic" green brochure for the "Wheel and Rock to Woodstock" bicycle tour one summer in the mid-90's, I decided that here was my chance to finally go to Woodstock while keeping my anatomy intact. So I did, and it ranks right up there among my most memorable weekends.

The tour, a two-day, 150-mile tour of New York State's Sullivan County Catskills was a fundraiser for the National Multiple Sclerosis Society. MS has lots of bikathons throughout the year, but this one was superb! The "Wheel and Rock to Woodstock" attracted over a thousand riders each year, and raised almost $500,000.

As a writer, and as a veteran of the New York City Bike Tour, the Tour de Torrington, the Massachusetts Tour de Cure, and a dozen other large-scale bike tours, I was commissioned by a national magazine to write this article about the tour, and about what it was like to finally arrive at "Woodstock."

As the tour concluded on the second day, I struggled up the final climb, and past the Woodstock monument – a granite slab with a bronze plaque commemorating the music festival site. I tried to picture what it must have been like a quarter century ago. The actual site of the music festival is simply an open field, perhaps a quarter mile square. The field is on the side of a hill (part of Max Yasgur's farm) and the stage was at the bottom of the hill. Wherever you sat, therefore, you would have a great view of the stage. The truth of the matter is that I couldn't really picture it. Try as I might, my imagination could not help me appreciate or comprehend the enormous magnitude of what had happened right here. I simply hadn't been there. I couldn't recreate the magic in my own mind, much less put it on paper for the magazine.

After sitting alone with my bike, recovering from the last big climb and trying to get "literary and philosophical" about the whole thing, I decided to give it up for a while and have lunch. After too much chicken and pasta, I tried once more. I walked the few hundred feet to the very top of the hill. I sat down on the grass, looked out over the entire field, and tried once again to imagine the sight, sound, and smell of a million stoned, wet hippies diggin' the music.

Nothing.

I lay back in the grass, sort of thrilled to be there, but discouraged that I couldn't find the feeling or the words to truly describe the magic.

A man was walking up the hill toward me. Tall and thin, bearded and balding, he appeared to be in his early forties, about my age at the time of this tour. His three kids reluctantly tagged along behind him. His son and two daughters were in their early teens. When they all reached the top of the hill, near where I lay, he stopped and turned to look down across the field. He took all three kids in a great bear hug, and pointed them in the direction he was looking.

"Kids," he said, "twenty-five years ago I sat right here on this very spot," he patted the ground, "with a million other kids, and saw the greatest concert of all time. Can you guys imagine a million hippies, with no TV, no food, no toilets, sittin' in the rain for three days, watching a concert of the biggest superstars of the decade? It was the best time I ever had in my whole life. It was really magic!" He sounded so proud to have brought his children to this spot, to maybe share a bit of his experience with them.

"Can we go down and get some more hot dogs now?" whined his son.

With a disgusted wave of his hand, the father dismissed his kids, and they trotted down the hill toward the food tents, laughing and poking fun at their dad to each other. The phrase "old fart" was clearly audible.

The man sat down a few feet from me. He didn't talk for a few minutes. Noticing that I was about his age and obviously sympathetic to his distress, he turned toward me and we had this brief conversation:

"They'll never know, will they?"

"No," I replied.

"I thought it would really mean something to them."

"They're too young," I said, "just as we were too young to appreciate our parents' views of the Korean conflict, World War II, the Great Depression, Frank Sinatra, and Uncle Miltie. The real awe stems from the experiences of the generation, not from the events themselves." It was the most profound thing I had thought of all day!

"Were you here in '69?" he asked me.

"No," I said, "but I think I can finally relate to what I missed."

I had, indeed, accomplished what I started. I had finally been to "Woodstock." For me, the magic had occurred at that exact moment, and I understood.

We sat on the hill for a few minutes longer, and we both cried a little. He, because he had been here, and I, because I had not.

We both wiped our eyes, walked down the hill, and ate more pasta. He found his kids. I got my picture taken at the monument, with a better understanding of, and appreciation for, the incredible significance of this simple patch of land.

ᛤ ᛤ ᛤ

Our Best Day Ever

By Geoffrey Husband

The best things in life are hard won. Raised in Britain, long a resident of France, the proprietor of Breton Bikes Cycling Holidays recalls his fondest ride "ever" in the mountains on the border between France and Spain.

The Ending . . .

Kate is about fifteen meters ahead, hair streaming, knees and elbows tucked in. A quick glance at the speedo shows thirty-five miles per hour. Braking hard for a hairpin, brakes squealing, then cranking the bike hard over, further and further, nothing scrapes, then upright again. The road drops steeply away, one in five, at a guess. Ahead of me Kate tucks down and lets out a whoop of excitement . . . 35, 40, 43 . . . I wear glasses but my eyes are streaming. Kate is a watery blur ahead . . . 46, 48, can I make 50? The bike gently shakes its head as if in answer and I sit up and let Kate go. Twenty minutes of wild descent has made us confident in our brakes and tires, but I have front panniers and, I suspect, a healthier sense of danger. I catch up five minutes later as the hill gently flattens, her hair a mess and a huge grin on her face.

"Brilliant!" she shouts, and we pull up at the side of the road and catch our breath. Our rims are too hot to touch and the tarmac is melting under the searing Spanish sun, but we are both cold. Now I know why the riders on "The Tour" stuff newspapers up their shirts.

The Beginning . . .

The day had started gently, a soft cool day in the little town of Arrette, France, where we had camped the night after a huge meal at the hotel in town. We were nervous – all the last day we had watched the mountains getting larger and larger, dominating the horizon halfway to the clouds. The first time I had seen real mountains, I'd been walking in Snowdonia, but these were giants. Arrette was at 150 meters, the top of Col Pierre – St. Martin pass was 1,800 meters, a climb of over 5,000 feet, and we had little idea of what we would find on the other side – in Spain.

We had chosen this pass back in England six months before, as part of the planning for our longest ever tour. Two weeks and 1,400 kilometers of hard cycling later we faced our biggest test. The ride to this point had hardened us up – we would never be fitter in our lives, and a glance at the map all those months before had shown us that the climb lasted for twenty-five kilometers, giving a quite manageable gradient of one in fifteen. So, we shook the early morning dew from the tent, packed our panniers and set off as the sun rose.

How wrong one can be! We soon picked up speed and instead of starting to climb we found ourselves cycling along a steep-sided valley. Five, then ten km and still we didn't climb. The mountains seemed to be wrapping all around us, blotting out the sun.

A little bridge, through a tiny copse of trees, a quick right-hand bend and then we saw it. Like Jacob's Ladder, soaring up in front of us, a road doing a passable impression of the side of a pyramid. Neither of us said anything, but there was a series of clatters as we both hit bottom gear and we began to climb. I will never forget those first 400 yards; all I could see was the tarmac directly below me as I honked in first gear. Blowed if I was giving up now! I could hardly believe it, but the road actually steepened around an outcrop of rock, then turned and leveled out slightly. I stopped, shaking and gasping for breath, turned 'round and was stunned to see Kate grinding up the hill not twenty meters behind me. She stopped and I grabbed a quick snap of her. I have that photograph in front of me now – it is a picture of exhaustion and despair. She looked like Tommy Simpson in that famous photo taken just before he died from heat exhaustion on the Ventoux. After she had gained enough breath she gasped, "It's no good, I'll never make it."

This was our nightmare, all this way and to fall at the first major hurdle. Were we going to have to freewheel back with our tail between our legs and find some easier way into Spain, i.e. a bus? We rested for five minutes, had a cuddle, and I confessed that I was exhausted, too. We could only see a few hundred meters further up the road as it wound its way up the mountain, but the gradient was certainly a little less. "Let's give it a go," said Kate and so we swung our legs over our saddles and began to climb.

That easier slope made all the difference, and our super-low bottom gears allowed us to settle into a gentle rhythm with enough breath left over to talk to each other. Some thoughtful soul had painted lines across the road every km, presumably for some insane cycle race, and had also marked the altitude. So as we climbed we had a good idea of how far we had got, and this helped us pace ourselves.

Soon we left the tree line behind and saw the mountain stretching ahead. Sheep grazed on the rough pasture in the distance. ("Wait a minute – they're not sheep, they're cows.") Suddenly the scale changed and the mountain looked twice as big. I could hear the gentle clanking of their bells echoing across the valley. Why were they clanking in time to my pedaling? It wasn't cowbells; it was my spokes making pinging noises as I pressed on the pedals! A quick inspection showed nothing amiss, but I listened with one ear for the snap of a spoke for the rest of the climb.

Every couple of kilometers we stopped and had a rest, gazing speechless at the scenery spreading before us, there's a chough, and another! These little crows pirouetted in front of us as if giving us our own personal aerobatics display. The top of the mountain was lost in the clouds, and below us we could see the tiny meandering road we had climbed.

Time to press on. The soft wet clouds engulfed us for a few hundred meters and then we emerged into brilliant sunshine, the top of the mountain invisible behind the slope. Nearly there, a helpful kilometer line told us we had only 800 meters to climb. Round a hairpin, then there it was! The ugliest half-built ski resort you have ever seen. Music blared from tinny speakers and a bar looking like an office block advertised "steak frits." We could have wept. No mention on the map, it was too new. So this was to be the summit, literally, of the day's achievement. We succumbed and sat and munched our dinner with an ice-cold beer. We were the only diners. What else would you expect at a ski resort in August?

The food revived us and there was a little further to the summit, so we mounted our steeds and wound our way from the monstrosity behind us. After 500 meters it was as if the ski resort had been swept from the face of the Earth. We were at the top, that thrilling, "brilliant" descent to come. Behind us spread the green mountains of France, ahead of us the Spanish border, marked by a tatty wooden barrier and diligently manned by a very bored-looking cow, not a human in sight. Beyond that, Spain, baked hard brown, tiny dark villages, and many more passes in the Cantabrian Mountains.

There would many adventures to come on other days. But none would ever match Our Best Day Ever.

⚲ ⚲ ⚲

Learn more about Geoff and Kate and Breton Bikes online at www.bretonbikes.com.

Spinning His Way Into History

By Jim Joyce

Cyclists' hearts are known to be bigger and stronger, in more ways than one.

This guy spins his wheels hour after hour, day after day, going absolutely nowhere, except into history. He is Dan Oshop, ice-cream shop proprietor, union electrician, tireless charity fundraiser, world bicycle traveler . . . and proud, one-time world record holder.

Before the crack of dawn on Friday, November 16, 2003, Oshop mounted an upright Life Fitness stationary bike in the window of his "Bruster's Old Fashioned Ice Cream & Yogurt Shop," a minute's bike ride from his Pittsburgh home and across the Monongahela River from whence stood the Homestead Works, once the world's largest steel mill. Sixty-one grueling hours later he ran out of steam, cranking his final pedal stroke, but not before shattering the previous record of sixty hours of continuous stationary cycling. While he faithfully stayed seated, news of his attempt to break the record sped into the pages of the local papers and across the television screens of Western Pennsylvania and adjacent states.

Though he hails from a neighborhood known as "Greenfield," Oshop is anything but green to cycling. The fifty-something, seasoned cyclist circled the world on his road bike in 2000. What is green, however, is the estimated $50,000 he has raised in his many cycling adventures over the years, starting with his first MS 150 Tour eighteen years ago.

"I was hooked," said Oshop, who's been biking miles by the thousands to help others ever since. He also turned the stationary ride into a fundraiser, this time for Katie's Fund, which fuels research into pediatric cancer prevention at Pittsburgh's UPMC Children's Hospital. One day after the event, he'd already raised $5K in pledges.

"I like cycling and I like raising money for charity, and that's why I do these things," said a strikingly upbeat, cordial Oshop, after being rousted from sleep for a phone interview at 8 P.M. the night after his ride. That's just twenty-five hours after the feat. But what's even more amazing is what lay ahead. "I just went to bed because I have to head off to Washington, D.C., at 2 A.M., so that I can start a job there at 6 A.M." This time he'll wear the hat of an electrician.

To be merciful, I suggested an interview at a better time, but Oshop insisted he would be fine and went on to relate the many highlights, and a few lowlights, of his historic ride.

"I didn't do anything special to prepare for the ride," he said, "though I did do an English century the Saturday before." He added with a chuckle, "What I really missed practicing was sleep deprivation!"

Oshop kept well fed during the ride and insisted on keeping his shop open for business. Slides of his world tour, videos, and chatting with friends and customers helped him pass the time. A second stationary bike was brought in so fellow cyclists could take turns riding alongside him, giving him encouragement. One kind soul even donated a satellite dish so the crew would not miss the Steelers game. The strict Guinness rules allowed him to break for just fifteen minutes every eight hours.

"During those breaks," said Oshop, "it was amazing how a twelve-minute nap would help."

Naps and hearty eating were keys to his success, he insisted. Occasionally, his crew would briefly encircle him with a sheet when he had to take care of – let's call it – urgent personal business, while he continued riding. He also slipped into the restroom during breaks. He recalled that one of the funniest moments of the ride resulted when an unexpected attack of stomach cramps caused him to call for the encircled sheet while he had to continue pedaling.

"That's one part I won't miss," laughed the cyclist.

Oshop recalls hitting the dreaded "wall" twice during the ride and fearing that he would not finish due to leg cramps, which eventually subsided. During the last few hours, he was in a "trance" of sorts.

"I felt like I was in a different place altogether at times. Sometimes, I wasn't sure of what was happening."

But he kept pedaling.

At 6:45 P.M. on Monday, November 18, Oshop surpassed sixty hours, the former mark reached by two men from South Africa, who had held the record for exactly one year, three weeks.

At sixty-one hours, however, he knew he could go no further than the 1,307 virtual miles on his odometer. "My butt was just so unbearably sore," he said, "and my legs hurt bad."

Except for the *Guinness Book's* certification, it was official. The Iron Man with a heart of gold, from the Steel City, would etch his name in the world's most renowned record book.

And so, as his interview wound down and he looked forward to further, precious sleep, Oshop pondered the idea of another such run for the record, should his ever be broken.

"This time I had no idea what I was getting into. Now I know. I would be better prepared. But would I ever do it a second time?" He paused for a moment, and then added with certainty, "I'd do it again for charity."

⏝ ⏝ ⏝

Afterword: Dan Oshop indeed set the world record that day and, afterwards, the *Guinness Book* officials certified it. However, before the next volume of the book was completed, another rider broke Dan's record, so he never saw his record in print. Time will tell whether he gives it another ride. But whatever he decides, Dan can be proud that he indeed held an official Guinness cycling record, and – even better – he won the hearts of his city.

Beyond The Streetcar. Way Beyond.

By Ted Katauskas

Both my grandfathers worked on the railroad, when "single track" was what you laid for a living. This contraption would no doubt turn their "roadie" grandson (the editor) into a "railroadie." By the sound of it, the author is already a convert.

When a veteran railbiker invited me for a ride in southern California last spring, here's what I had to do: Fly to Spokane. Rent a truck. Drive to Coeur d'Alene, Idaho. Disassemble and box a pedal-powered locomotive. Cart it back to Spokane. Fly to San Diego. Rent a four-wheel-drive. Drive to the Mexican border. Reassemble my rig on a ribbon of rusted rail in the Sonoran Desert. Show the owner of the decommissioned line proof of a $1.5 million group liability insurance policy, lest we derail on a Gold Rush-era trestle and join the twisted freight cars littering the dry creek bed at the bottom of the Carrizo Gorge.

All this, I was told, was pretty much what you had to do if you wanted to railbike, which would explain why virtually nobody in this adrenaline-addicted world has ever seen – much less ridden – one.

But then something incredible happened. Olympia-based Railbike Tours Inc. (www.railbike.com), the nation's only commercial railbike tour operator, began offering two- to four-hour railbike excursions on the Willamette Shore Trolley Line between Willamette Park and Lake Oswego, Washington. Since I'm one of the few (perhaps the only) experienced railbikers in town, I took one of the company's experimental tandem models out for a spin.

On an overcast Monday morning, I met Craig Sheley, Railbike Tours' operations manager, at the Southwest Carolina Street trolley crossing. I took my seat beside him on what looked like a bed frame with bicycle wheels: two recumbents joined side-by-side with sections of Schedule 40 plumbing pipe.

You would think two guys zipping along a railroad track on a bed frame would turn a few heads. You would think. But people just jogged by, absorbed in their music or walking their dogs. The homeless people camped in Powers Marine Park didn't even look up from their newspapers. Landscapers finishing the front lawn of a multi-million-dollar mansion just a few feet from the tracks were likewise oblivious. Then I realized we were invisible because we weren't making any noise, other than a few clacks and whirring gears.

Since I was on the outboard bike, Sheley warned me about the "pucker factor" of the first trestle. Before I saw it, I smelled the creosote. Then the forest to my left fell away, revealing a sheer drop to the rocky shore of the Willamette seventy-five feet below.

"Here's the best part," Sheley said.

We downshifted into Elk Rock Tunnel, banked right, then left. For a quarter mile, we were floating, flying though space in absolute blackness. Senseless, except for the wind on our cheeks.

🚲 🚲 🚲

This piece first appeared in Willamette Week *(www.wweek.com).*

GREASY FOOD, DRESS SOCKS
AND THE MOUNTAINS

By Bradley Swink

The year is 1990; the temperature, a balmy ninety degrees; the terrain, the unforgiving Laurel Mountains of Southwestern Pennsylvania. The author has no idea of what's to follow when he's invited to join a tough band of cyclists for a training ride – led by a multi-sport athlete destined for greatness.

It was raining when I set off from my hometown of Connellsville to the nearby mountains in which we planned to ride. The forecasters claimed the wet weather would abate near nine, so I thought little of the water cascading over my secondhand, Scandinavian-beige Volvo sedan.

With the flat road turning upward, my faithful old car howled and roared with displeasure, and searched for a lower gear. As I continued to put miles between the comforting hugs of home and the then-unknown climbs of the Laurel Mountains, the sky and road became a bit kinder. The gentler terrain, though, seemed nothing but a charade, for I felt certain the suffering would soon commence.

Mac Martin waited for me in the parking lot of Indian Head's only breakfast house, a dirty, smoky joint Mac aptly called the "grease pit." Though it had been our first meeting, I was already well acquainted with the legendary and eccentric ways of William Mac Martin, a bike racer and multi-sport athlete who would later become a multiple world champion biathlete and triathlete, as well as my daily training partner.

Joe Ross, a mutual racing friend, had the brilliant idea of meeting Mac in the mountains for the training ride. More brilliant still, he also invited me.

Joe and I were lied to and told the ride would be an easy parade through the lowlands with a climb or two thrown in to stretch the legs. Looking back on that ride, I can't recall even a single pedal stroke turning with any resemblance of ease.

As we retreated to the innards of the restaurant, I couldn't help but notice Mac's glaring disregard for popular dress. He wore navy blue, acrylic dress socks, pulled just above the ankle; black and neon yellow shorts from a Mike Fraysee-managed team; a racing top bearing the markings of South American sponsors (at least one size too small, presumably stolen or forcibly taken) and finally a well-worn pair of black loafers. All damn inappropriate, I thought at the time.

Once inside I was overcome by an intolerable wave of hot air, the smell of grease rode its swell. Joe sat near a window fighting off columns of sun and wisely ate as if the meal might be his last. Next to Joe sat a fourteen-year-old, reed-thin Max Bergholz, who was devouring the largest bowl of cereal I may have ever seen.

Though quite young and exceedingly timid looking, Max was already a member of Mac's "Frequent Survivors Club," a limited band of riders who routinely met with no other purpose but to traverse the region's many mountain passes.

I put down a coffee-stained menu, ordered and later enjoyed a jalapeno and cheddar omelet, copiously topped with cayenne and Red Hot, black coffee, wheat toast and a handsome pile of Pennsylvania bacon. The breakfast of bloated, soon-to-get-dropped champions, I later thought.

We drove the short distance from the restaurant to Mac's mountain cabin, filled water bottles, evacuated bowels and bladders and bolted. Max and I rode bareheaded, not uncommon in 1990, despite Mac's incessant badgering for headgear.

The treeless road offered no respite from the glaring sun, as the hard right from Mac's gravel drive instantly and savagely turned skyward. I immediately gulped the ninety-degree air, and easily identified Max as the dangerman of the group. As he effortlessly danced up the day's first climb, we were collectively left to fight for his disappearing wheel. The teenager's powerful yet fluid surges were the kind only a pure climber could dole out.

Meanwhile, red-faced and sweating like an acre of pigs, Mac answered every attack that came his way, while I was at my limit to sit on. Wearing an unremitting mask of torment, simply sitting on took every ounce of fitness and gamesmanship I had.

It wasn't until the day's last major climb, the old ascent out of Ohiopyle State Park, that young Max revealed signs of discontent. At the foot of the climb Mac punched hard on his pedals, quickly opening a ten-meter gap. Joe and I looked to a weary Max to chase, but it was obvious his daylong campaign of aggression had finally taken its toll.

In a selfless show of diplomacy, I shifted into my 23, stood on the pedals, and fought my bike, lungs and legs in an attempt to arrest the flyer quickly disappearing up the road. Unfortunately, Mac was soon out of sight, I was near death, Max was clinging to my wheel and Joe was off the back. Hopeless, I thought, before wisely sitting up.

An hour or so later, as we crested the false-flat leading to the Martin family compound, I realized I was utterly pounded. I coughed uncontrollably, had no appetite to speak of, carried a clammy film over my entire body and carelessly threw my new carbon fiber bike in the yard. The curtain had fallen on our daylong ride.

Under pillars of a still unforgiving bloody sun, and above the din of my thumping head, I somehow heard Mac shout, "Same time tomorrow?" Reeling like a drunk on a two-day binge, eager for one more, I couldn't help but respond, "Sure."

🚲 🚲 🚲

Recalling his many tough but memorable rides in the mountains with Mac Martin, Mr. Swink notes: "That ride, and subsequent mountain rides with Mac, were almost always 100 miles or more. I suspect we were intrigued by the notion of riding so far and so long on such grueling terrain. The rides would usually last seven or more hours (depending upon the route). After those mountain rides, we would nap for an hour or two, then run for another two hours."

Riding Buddies

By Cathy Dion

Many a friendship is built on bicycling and, like a bike that's well cared for, they survive even the toughest of rides.

I had not seen Ron for almost two years. No excuses really, although I had moved out of the area and he had gone on an extended bike tour around the U.S. Before he left he had sold or stored nearly all of his possession and planned on living at the Veterans Affairs Hospital on his return. Indeed, that is where he landed. In the meantime he developed Alzheimer's disease.

For twelve years we were the most compatible riding companions. Even though he was in his sixties when we first met, our paces and styles of riding were very similar. He liked the idea of bike touring, too. We took many two and three-day trips together as well as longer expeditions. He spoke fondly of how perfect our travels were; of how the weather was always just right and aside from a flat tire here and there no disasters ever occurred. Oh, sure, we rode through our share of rain and cold but our rides were always enjoyable. He loved being out on the open road, as do I.

He is fairly conservative in his political views. A veteran of Korea, his Army stories were often repeated. Born in England, he moved with his parents when he was three to New Zealand. At fifteen he decked his father and crewed on a yacht to Australia. There he learned the crafts of shipbuilding and sail making. He made his way to the United States at the age of eighteen and promptly became a citizen. After the war he married, had two sons, divorced, hung out with the rich yachting set in Marin, crewed yachts and built boats.

In his forties he took up cycling and became a champion time trialist. He knew Joe Breeze, mountain bike pioneer, and in fact still owns one of Joe's original aluminum mountain bikes. He has done all of his tours on that bike.

In the late 1980s Ron settled in Calistoga, California, which is when I met him.

One morning a few years ago, he was supposed to pick me up. We were headed out to the ocean in Marin County for a ride. It was not like him to be late. "Maybe he lost track of time at the coffee shop," I thought. I pedaled over and found him joking with friends at his morning hangout, his long narrow fingers wrapped around a steaming mug.

"Hi, Cath," he said as I walked in.

"Hey, I thought were going for a ride. You were going to pick me up?"

"Oh," he said. "I thought we were meeting here. Where we goin' again?"

"Out to the Cheese Factory."

"Roight," he mused in his thick Kiwi accent. "Want a cup of coffee?"

"No thanks. We'd better get going."

"Roight." He chugged down the last dregs in his cup. His friends wished us well and we were off on another beautiful ride.

In June of 2000 the two of us went on an Alaskan voyage. It was a dream trip for me and for Ron, well, "I'll follow you," he had always said. So, I made all the arrangements; the ferryboat up the Inside Passage, several train trips, a hotel in Seattle and campground in Skagway and the Yukon. Several times during our adventure I saw signs that maybe his mind was failing. Once, just minutes after I'd repaired the camp stove, we sat down to a hot home-cooked meal and he said: "It's a good thing I fixed the stove, eh?"

Hmm. Sometimes he would take off on his bike when we were camped in Skagway and I worried if he would remember how to get back. But he always returned, and when I asked him where he had been he replied, "Down by the docks watching the boats." He loved the sea and boats, large and small.

Towards the end of our trip we split up in Bellingham. He wanted to ride his bike back to Calistoga and I had to catch a train and return to work. After a few weeks his friends and family started calling me and asking had I heard from Ron? No. He never wrote to anybody. Finally he arrived back home safe and sound. Then in October he took off on a cross-country bicycle tour. I bid him farewell and that was the last I saw of him. After a year and a half he returned and took up residence at the V.A.

Now I was finally going to visit him. I was a bit apprehensive. Having worked in health care for some twenty years, I had seen many people with Alzheimer's in various stages of deterioration. I wondered if he would remember me. I worried that he would be a different person altogether.

Many efforts by the friendly staff at the V.A. Hospital had assured me that Ron would show up at his appointed time. A final call to his ward and he soon came wheeling his silver steed up to the building where I waited. A security officer accompanied him. He looked the same, tall and lanky. His skinny white legs barely filled his sagging, Lycra shorts. He was wearing a new, bright red Pearl Izumi jacket. He donned the same helmet. His cleats clicked happily on the lobby floor and we hugged.

"Hi, Cath," he said in his thick Kiwi accent. He remembered! We were so glad to see each other.

"Want a cup of coffee?" he asked.

"Sure," I said. While we sipped we caught up and reminisced. He told me all about his trip around the country.

"But you know," said Ron, "none of that can compare to our trip to Alaska."

He spoke in great detail of our experiences there, especially camping out for four days on the upper deck of the M.V. Matanuska as it slowly pushed its way up the coast. He recalled seeing trees full of bald eagles. He remembered all the bear scat along the lonely Klondike Highway. "Meals on Wheels" is what they call bicycle tourists up there. He drained his cup. "Well, shall we go for a spin?"

"I'm ready. My bike is in the truck."

"Where we goin'?"

"Oh, I thought we'd head up to Lake Hennessy on the Silverado Trail."

"Roight. I'll follow you, dear."

We sailed out past old stonewalls, past miles and miles of carefully tended vineyards, roads we used to ride years before. It was like old times and we matched pace.

"Beautiful day, isn't it?" I remarked.

"Gorgeous!" he exclaimed. "Where we goin'?"

"Up the trail."

"Roight. I'll follow you."

Yep, it was just like old times.

🚲 🚲 🚲

CROSS COUNTRY TANDEM TRIP:
A JOURNAL

By Rhona & Dave Fritsch

This piece includes selections from the amusing "he said, she said" chronicle of a husband-wife team's cross-country tandem ride (3,710 miles over forty-seven days). The Fritsch's live in Keyser, West Virginia.

Rhona and I began our great tandem adventure in Washington State and finished in New Jersey. Rhona accepted the major responsibility of compiling a journal each night. Her narrative is typed in regular print. In the interests of historical accuracy (wink), I added comments, in *italics*.

— Dave Fritsch

DAY 1
Tuesday, June 18
Anacortes Island, WA to Rockport, WA (71 miles)

What a beautiful day to begin our trip! Not a drop of rain, cool and sunny.

We couldn't get near the water at the ferry landing in Anacortes so we went to a nearby boat-launching ramp and had an official "bike launching!" We passed through such a variety of terrain today, from the seacoast, through farmlands, along the beautiful Skagit River valley, to the foothills of the Northern Cascade Mountains. Pine-forested ranges and snow-covered peaks surround us. The Skagit River itself is beautiful, fairly wide, a swift-flowing, sparkling green reflection of its forested banks. We camped right on its banks.

The flora has been interesting, very large and lush. Every plant seems oversized, from the trees to the roadside shrubs, ferns and flowers. There is a familiar flower I'm anxious to identify. It's like our eastern Blue Bells, but the "bells" are amazingly large.

The fauna thus far has consisted of deer skittering across the road, and numerous bald eagles (*much* to Dave's delight). We see many of them circling above and hear others screaming in the forest. When we were driving with Ross, I saw what I thought was someone's remote control helicopter, but it was an eagle hovering over its prey.

Such friendly people so far (one day). Everyone is interested in and amazed at what we're doing. We purchased a glass of lemonade from two girls at a small stand and made a bonus purchase of four daisies for eight cents.

While eating lunch in a "Subway," we met a tandem rider/bicycle shop employee. He's a serious cyclist and is preparing for a 200-mile race; his female stoker just qualified to compete in the "Iron Man" race. Locals were helpful in directing us to the county park for camping. Also, I hope today's vehicular traffic is the norm. Drivers were extremely polite and gave us lots of room. Only one dog attacked us today, and one spray of HALT was sufficient. What a fantastic first day!

DAY 2
Wednesday, June 19
Rockport, WA to Washington Pass (73 miles)

Today was certainly a contrast to yesterday! It was probably the most challenging climb we have ever done, approximately forty miles up to Washington Pass. We went from hot (I wore a crop-top) to snow banks several feet high. The day ended in a wilderness campsite and we were glad to have that!

We took way too long in the morning to get started, not yet efficient at packing, dealing with laundry, and partaking in a leisurely breakfast. Our destination was eighty-six miles away, with no services along the way. I bought some snacks and we started out, disregarding several locals' (and other cyclists') surprise at what we were attempting. I think from now on I'll believe the locals; it's just that we always assume they're not looking at things from a cyclist's point of view.

The climb began along the lakes and reservoirs created by the Diablo and Ross Dams. The water is the most beautiful emerald green, just like pictures I've see of Jamaica. Only the power lines spoiled the views. We continued to climb for hours, leaving most signs of civilization behind.

It became obvious that we were not going to reach our destination of Mazama on the other side of Washington Pass, and also that we weren't going to have enough food (I hope to never see another granola bar.). Water, we were okay on, because a highway crew let us fill our bottles from their supply.

Dave wanted to stop and camp far down on the western side of the pass and renew our efforts in the morning. But I held a whip over him (that's his version) and made us keep going. I knew that without food I'd have an extremely difficult time doing the climb in the morning. However, if we could at least get over the pass, then the next day would be downhill . . . that I could handle without nourishment! (The next day, Dave told me he was very uncertain about whether or not we could get over the pass by nightfall, and if we didn't, there would be no way to keep warm at that altitude. For once he was worried and I wasn't.) So, we continued to walk/ride and finally reached Washington Pass at about 8:30 P.M. By that time the sun was setting and it was freezing! Dave said I wouldn't want to know the temperature.

Snow was piled several feet high in places. As difficult as the climb up had been, the three miles we descended (approximately 2,000 feet drop in elevation) was really hard on Dave – very cold and windy. We stopped at a forest service campsite (nothing but pit toilets) where we quickly made camp, hung our remaining muffins in a tree for protection from bears, and collapsed. I changed my bike pants, but otherwise just layered on more clothes and huddled in my sleeping bag, even tying up the "mummy hood." Actually, it wasn't too bad inside the tent.

The day's scenery and views were spectacular and well worth the effort. The Cascade Mountains are very aptly named for the many waterfalls. These northern Cascades remind us very much of our ride to Lake Kootenay in British Columbia; I assume it is all the same basic range of mountains.

I'm very proud of how I handled today's experience; I viewed it as an adventure and at no time was I upset or worried (as soon as I knew Dave was following my plan). We had water and I had Dave, my trusty Boy Scout. I knew we could handle anything! With only two muffins to tide us over for dinner and breakfast, we thought only of each other, no snarling and grabbing at the food. Dave let me have most of one for dinner, while he said his body was "feasting on fat cells." (I don't know if I need a new pen or if it's just too cold for this one. I'm sure when we're climbing the Appalachians in August we'll remember this cold weather with longing.)

DAY 3
Thursday, June 20
Washington Pass to Okanagan, WA (67 miles)

We left the "Land of the Early Winters" this morning and immediately descended for another five miles. Mysteriously, there was no sign of the whip Rhona used on me last night. This morning, she kept pulling on the bit, wanting to slow down. We had breakfast in a "general store" in Mazama, which appeared to be part of a dude ranch.

The sandwiches were very good. The wind was in our face until midday and, as promised by locals, the desert began. The climb up Loup Pass was much easier than yesterday's climb and the descent was great. On the way into Okanagan we passed irrigated apple orchards. If it isn't irrigated, then it's sagebrush. Since there was no opportunity to clean up last night, we stopped at a motel tonight.

The tandem is working fine, although the camping gear gets heavier by the day.

Although I've been advised not to include a discussion of food in a journal, I just have to say more about the Mazamo Store. It had such a neat atmosphere . . . Mother Earth/L.L. Bean type, with homegrown/natural products and employees in Birkenstocks. I had the most fabulous orange scones for breakfast! We met two more people who had cycled cross-country. One was the postal employee who didn't even charge me for a mailing envelope to send items back home. People continue to be incredibly friendly. One retired couple from Florida (they had lived in McDowell County, West Virginia, years ago) stopped on the roadside to take our picture and get our name and address. Our WV license plate had attracted their attention.

Motorists continue to be courteous. One highway worker held traffic to let us pass (going uphill!) and we even saw a sign warning cyclists of a hazard.

DAY 4
Friday, June 21
Okanagan, WA to Republic, WA (72 miles)

There was only one way to characterize today's ride . . . headwind, headwind, headwind! It was a fifty-nine-mile gradual ascent but the wind made even level and downhill sections difficult to pedal. I was whipped and, of course, Dave takes the brunt of the wind. We stopped at the Regal Fruit Co-op, hoping to buy a few apples, and the woman didn't charge us for them and also told us how her children did a coast-to-coast trip. Everywhere we go people tell us how they or someone they know cycled cross-country.

An older gentleman stopped and offered us assistance when we were walking up the mountain, and I explained that I was looking for an outdoor restroom! We saw him again at the store near the top of Wauconda Summit and he expressed such an interest in our trip. This is one of the highlights of the trip . . . meeting and talking to so many locals and other cyclists.

We *moteled* for the second night in a row; we're getting in so late. I blame Dave for not getting up and getting on the road earlier!

A Rottweiler that meant business chased us today, but Rhona was accurate again with her first spray of HALT – mighty impressive in light of the strong wind at the time. She is now "two for two." I hope the word spreads to dogs further up along the route: "Stay away from the funny looking bicycle with the two people."

Deer are *everywhere*. Terrain was the same as yesterday, desert-like mountains, sagebrush, actually very boring. Unfortunately, I fear that most of America's heartland will be similar to this. Four days in Washington and so far no rain.

DAY 5
Saturday, June 22
Republic, WA to Colville, WA (54 miles)

I spoke too soon, rain all day (until we had committed to paying for a motel room) but it was never heavy. It was cold up on Sherman Pass but for once Dave had gotten out of bed early enough and we weren't stranded at the top at night! We met Andrew and Allen, a father-son team cycling to Boston. Another friendly retired couple stopped to talk to us and even offered us food and a place to stay.

I've discovered a similarity between cycling in Washington and in West Virginia. It's *still* unnerving to look in your mirror and see a huge logging truck barreling down on you. These trucks are much bigger and are carrying huge logs. The forests that we cycled through today are exactly how I pictured Washington and Oregon – dense forests of tall "pointy" pines covering the mountainsides. We rode through the area of the 1988 White Mountain fire.

Rhona had problems getting her clipless pedals to release today, meaning she could not dismount from the bike. She should be able to just twist her foot out. She told me I should be able to "feel her power" when she tried, prompting visions of ninety-five-pound "Power Ranger Rhona" in my mind. I fixed them tonight. The temperature at the top of Sherman Pass was thirty-eight degrees and it was raining. We had lunch under a small roof at the pass with four other cyclists, two of whom were going cross-country.

The moment was the type of encounter I had hoped for: Adventure seekers enjoying the companionship enhanced by a shared experience.

Later, at the Columbia River, we were walking across the pedestrian walkway. Rhona hummed out loud. I thought it somewhat incongruous that she was crossing the "Far Away" River, about 4,000 miles from home, with only a bicycle to get her home. And yet she was ambling along like she was walking on the street in front of our home.

DAY 6
Sunday, June 23
Colville, WA to Newport, ID (96 miles)

Very poor directions on the map in several places today. One time we finally flagged down a passing motorist for directions. It was much rainier today but there were no high passes so we made good time and mileage. We passed through the Kalispell Indian Reservation. We're told this is grizzly country – some troublesome bears from Yellowstone are relocated here. I'm not eating very nutritiously. As I feared might happen, too many of our meals are at "burger joints."

As I had hoped, many of our meals are at "burger joints."

I get french fries and ice cream, actually worse for me than a burger. I realize now I can simply ask for a cheeseburger, minus the burger! We completed Washington State at 8 P.M. on June 23 after five days of riding and 433 miles.

DAY 7
Monday, June 24
Newport, ID to Clark Fork, MT (70 miles)

Torrential downpour this morning and early afternoon, very worrisome and unpleasant. Nice bike route over Lake Pend Oreille (Idaho) via an old bridge (the motor vehicles use the adjoining new bridge). We had a late start again since it rained in the night and everything was soaked, making packing a hassle. Seemed like slow riding too, although not much uphill. We do seem to stop frequently to add or remove clothing. The lake was gorgeous, reminded us so much of Uncle Ross's place on Kootenay Lake in British Columbia.

Ants in my pants! The "behind a bush" roadside bathroom facilities leave something to be desired.

Spent the night in a hostel on a ranch. It was a nice little cabin surrounded by lots of farm animals. We walked around with a cyclist, Ed, who had been a bike messenger in San Francisco and was now staying in the next cabin. A colt had been born that morning. He was learning to nurse. Pigs roamed free, came right up to nuzzle around the bike, so we brought everything into the cabin.

I had to swat one of the pigs in the snout to keep it out of a pannier, but it didn't seem to care.

We saw signs in store windows and in yards saying "We Support Logging" or "This family Supported By the Timber Industry."

DAY 10
Thursday, June 27
Olney, MT to Lake McDonald, Glacier Park (62 miles)

Today is our daughter Kelly's birthday. We made great time to Whitefish, beautiful weather. We stopped at a bike shop and got advice on the logistics of sending home all the camping gear. The bike is just too heavy and wind resistant for us to make good time. It takes us till 9 P.M. to finish ninety miles and that's too long in the saddle. Also, Dave must use so much strength and effort to steer and control it. And camping requires so much longer to set up/break camp. It won't be too bad to ride long hours if we're pulling into a motel.

More torrential rain – streets flooded; we took brief refuge under an awning of a little place on the highway but had to continue on eventually. I finally got some vegetables! Hot, steamed, fresh veggies – *heaven*. While on the street packing our gear to send home, a retired school principal stopped and talked at length. He's interested in tandems and cycled across Africa last year. He had lots of advice for us. He told us not to worry about getting a motel room; they'll somehow find room for cyclists.

"Ask a farmer if he has a place for you," he said, making it sound so effortless. He even gave us his card in case we needed help in Montana. We stayed at the Lake McDonald Lodge in Glacier.

The interior of the lodge was spectacular. We had a lot of company in front of the huge fireplace.

DAY 11
Friday, June 28
Lake McDonald, MT to Browning, MT (70 miles)

Only the spectacular scenery made today bearable. I could not find a comfortable position on the seat no matter how I shifted; it was agony by afternoon. Also, it was very cold over Logan Pass in Glacier, plus we hit a hailstorm as we headed down the east side. It was painful, especially for Dave, who can't turn his face away as I can. We began at 7:45 A.M. and reached the top of the pass at 11:08 A.M. (cyclists must be off the west side of Going-to-the Sun Road by 11:00 A.M. due to heavy vehicular traffic). Phenomenal views and snow banks many feet high. The Visitors Center was closed. It was snowed in. We were surprised by how few (two) cyclists we saw, then read that the road just opened last weekend.

We had another long six-mile climb outside the park and then up, down, up, down. The road down was very winding and narrow with blind curves. I was not happy with our speed, and some whimpering did occur! We then crossed the Blackfeet Indian Reservation and stayed in a low-cost, no frills motel. I asked the owner if I could lay our clothes out in the back yard to dry, as the wind and sun would dry them in minutes. He said he had an eighty-five-pound pit bull in the backyard! So he put our clothes in his own dryer. People are so nice to us.

We took the "Mother of All Shortcuts" to Browning. We not only avoided a climb, but also took advantage of a twenty-five-miles-per-hour tailwind. By standing up we could coast for a mile without even pedaling. At dinner we sat next to a unique cross-country cyclist. He would cycle for a while, then stop and work to earn money enough to go on. He plans to go to Maine and then to New York to see the Statue of Liberty. He is pulling a trailer with about 100 pounds of equipment. He planned to go another thirty miles to Cutback before dark.

DAY 12
Saturday, June 29
Browning, MT to Chester, MT (104 miles)

Dave let me buy cherries from a roadside stand! I rigged up an ingenious method for carrying them and eating as we rode. With no daytime speed limit, riding through Montana has not been as pleasant as Washington. Many drivers are less courteous also. The white roadside crosses, which mark highway fatalities, are everywhere, even on long straightaways, with no trees or poles to hit. It must be head-on collisions involving speed and alcohol. There were signs about giving up alcohol all over the reservation. We passed through Devon, Montana, population thirteen. There was a Frontier Bar, a grain silo, and a signpost with about four family names on it. It makes Babb, Montana look positively metropolitan! We had a flat tire on the prairie.

The performance GT-K tire failed after only 1,000 miles.

We began to see prairie dogs; saw a scruffy mule deer. The bird life has been amazing ever since we began this trip. Being on a bicycle and traveling through desolate or sparsely populated areas has enabled us to hear such beautiful songs. Today we saw ten to twelve of what looked like pelicans – though we knew they couldn't be – and a similar brown bird.

We were lucky tonight. We were planning to ride on to Rudyard because we were feeling good and the tailwind was pushing us along at twenty miles per hour. I mentioned it to the dinner waitress in Chester and she said it was no longer open. So we checked in Chester's two motels and there was only one opening. We ended up paying for a suite with a kitchenette. It would have been sixty more miles to the next stop!

DAY 13
Sunday, June 30
Chester, MT to Harlem, MT (105 miles)

Much hotter weather today. Blazing sun, flat, less wind. We completed fifty-five miles before noon. We passed and were passed repeatedly by trains. One engineer gave us a big wave twice. My feet are bothering me after about seventy-five miles because of constant pressure on the pedals.

I wanted to go on to the next town, a distance of forty-three more miles, but Dave claims, "Cooler heads prevailed." I was happy we did stop, though, because the Olympic gymnastic trials were on TV.

DAY 15
Tuesday, July 2
Glasgow, MT to Poplar, MT (73 miles)

Another day of headwinds and temperatures over 100 degrees. We were hoping to sail quickly across the plains and are quite disappointed. Of course, my first thought is that we'll never get to Ocean City, New Jersey, in time to vacation with the family. It's hard to keep enough liquids in us, just like in Colorado last summer. I can't stand to drink warm or hot water, so I have begun buying bottled water when we stop and forcing myself to drink it while it's cold. Many towns have water that tastes horrible.

We stopped in Wolf Point to get spare tires and to remove the drum brake. Dave will add more about that later. While he was working on the bike, I lay in the backyard and enjoyed the clouds, wind chimes, songbirds, and even a rainbow when there wasn't a drop of moisture anywhere. Lots of hymns come to mind, like "This Is My Father's World." We planned to stay in Poplar because Colbertson was too far, but along the way two people told us it wasn't a very safe place, that it is known as "Stab City" due to the violence. But they said if we didn't camp or go to the bars we'd be okay. The people we met in Poplar were the same friendly type we've become accustomed to. We conversed over dinner with the ex-mayor and a farmer. They helped us get motel reservations for the next two nights.

Al's Bike Shop turned out to be a friendly, retired man running a one-room shop in his basement. He's been doing this for sixty years. He had to in order to keep his ten children provided with bicycles. He sold us two tires for seven dollars each, and also helped me take off the drum brake. Since we didn't have the special tool, we had to jury rig a tool, something I think he has done many times before. Al was married for more than fifty years, but his wife died years ago after receiving a heart transplant in 1982. I think Al takes care of the neighborhood kids' bikes and the neighbors take care of him. One lady stopped to check on what he had for supper.

One bank thermometer read 102 degrees while the one across the street read 112. I think 112 was more accurate.

DAY 17
Thursday, July 4
Williston, ND to Parshall, ND (93 miles)

Shall I describe a day in hell? Even worse winds than yesterday, hill after hill after hill, another ruined tire, and a fifty-mile stretch with absolutely no services, not even a bush to go behind! However, since I've decided to focus only on the positive aspects of this journey, we were blessed with cloud cover the entire day, no bugs, and a very kindly farm lady who let us fill our water bottles from her well. The woman acted like it was an everyday occurrence. Even her "guard" dog rolled over for a belly scratch on the front porch. She seemed like an angel to us. I doubt that Dave could have gone much further without water. Also, we had a wonderful lunch at a marina ...homemade vegetable soup and Saskatoon berry-rhubarb pie. Mmmm. Made me think of Mom.

The headwinds were brutal today, twenty-five to thirty-five miles per hour. The tandem was hard to handle when the winds would shift and catch the panniers. We were frequently forced to push the bike as we became more fatigued. Rhona was sometimes unable to push the bike by herself because of the strong winds. At one point while following her up the road, I noticed the rear tire (Performance GT-K) had worn a hole through and the Kevlar fibers were pushing out of the tread.

I was shocked by the premature failure since the tire had ridden only about 300 miles. We had to change the tire along the road, near the top of a hill, while a thunderstorm approached. It was a very discouraging day. Our response was to just keep going, even if going meant walking at three miles per hour.

DAY 18
Friday, July 5
Parshall, ND to Minot, ND (64 miles)

It's amazing the things stokers will do to prevent boredom! I've invented license plate games that are too embarrassing to describe, I can recite the alphabet as quickly backwards as forwards, and I rewrote the lyrics to "This Land is Your Land." Here it goes ....

> *As we were biking that hilly byway,*
> *I saw above me the windy skyway;*
> *I saw before me that endless highway,*
> *This land is going to kill us both.*

Yesterday a man in a decrepit car inched along the highway with us and serenaded us with "A Bicycle Built for Two" through the passenger side, front window.

The wind teased us by blowing in our direction for fifteen miles then abruptly changed and became a head/cross wind for most of the day. We had another flat tire just outside Minot, where we were going to a bike shop to purchase two new tires. So we spent a boring hour and a half in a bike shop (reminded me of my childhood in fabric stores).

We spent a quick, fascinating hour and a half in a bike shop while they replaced the front derailleur (reminded me of my childhood in toy stores).

I've decided there are four categories of pain of the rear end. First is the bone pain, where the actual pelvic bones hurt. Then you have the soft tissue pain, which is self-explanatory. Next there is nerve pain, when you're sitting on a nerve that shoots pain up through your lower back and it extends down to your knee. Finally there is the "sitting-on-a-saddle-sore" (pimple) pain, also self-explanatory. Oh, yes, I forgot the regular old pain-in-the-a ___ , which is how you view the captain when you're flying down hill too fast or swerving in and out of traffic!

I'm not too happy with today's progress. I see my beach vacation slipping away. I haven't talked to daughter Kelly since her birthday. There's so much I'd like to share with her but I got her answering machine when I called her.

We bought three Specialized Armadillo tires to try to end our problems with tire failures. The bike shop owner crammed our bike in for work even though the shop was very busy and it was late in the afternoon. Bicycle people consistently bend over backwards to help us whenever they can on this trip.

DAY 19
Saturday, July 6
Minot, ND to Carrington, ND (132 miles)

A new personal best! Our nineteenth day was a breeze, both literally and figuratively. We got started at 6:30 A.M. in order to beat the heat and to get lots of miles in to make up for yesterday. But we had lots of cloud cover all day and finally the wind was headed in approximately our direction! We rode forty miles before 9 A.M. The terrain has really changed; western North Dakota was dry and very hilly, even though we skirted north of the Badlands. The eastern half, however, is level, fertile farmland. It's strange but there are virtually no mosquitoes here; we've decided that the east to west winds blew them all back to Montana (Saco especially, since they claim to be The Mosquito Capital of the World!).

Yesterday and today we felt as though we were in a Hitchcock movie. Birds all but attacked us, swooping and diving as we rode past their nests in the wetlands along the road. We're glad to be wearing helmets! I think I have some sun poisoning – itchy bumps where I burned.

Before Dave writes his comments and I'm accused of violence, let me state that I smacked Captain Dave on the rear when he made two quick U-turns, then almost wrecked (with traffic coming), just to get a Mentos candy he dropped!

Stoker Rhona's sun poisoning seems to have affected her visual perception and made her emotionally volatile! Today, she dropped a handful of Mentos candy. The resulting clatter startled me, causing an almost imperceptible swerve of the bicycle. Fortunately, there were no motor vehicles in the surrounding three-county area. My soothing voice calmed her and she responded with a love tap on the back.

DAY 25
Friday, July 12
Milaca, MN to Stillwater, MN (121 miles)

Had some rain today and the terrain got much more hilly after we crossed the St. Croix River into Wisconsin. Dave didn't think very highly of the route, and my knees didn't like it either! We hit the 2,000-mile mark today! Stillwater is an attractive town; reminds me of Pittsburgh's Station Square only there are many more quaint shops and exclusive stores. The riverfront looked lovely from afar and it would have been nice to walk around downtown, but our motel was at least three miles away and after showering and eating, all we want to do is collapse, not sight-see.

The Montana and Wisconsin fire departments have an excellent procedure for locating rural properties. Each house has a metal plate (like a license plate) mounted on a post by their driveway, bearing a fire identification number.

DAY 35
Monday, July 22
87 miles Gibson City, IL to Lafayette, IN (87 miles)

Rode for a while this morning with John and Larry, whom we met last night at our motel. They're going to spend a few days at the Olympics. John is a dairy farmer (taught us about corn) and a high school wrestling coach and Larry (an engineer) was a high school wrestler who competed in state-level competition. We joked that we'd look for them in the men's cycling event. We rode into Indiana about 11 A.M. After a while, it had a little more variety than Illinois, some gentle grades and more trees. Rode onto Purdue's campus enough to get a picture. Lafayette is large and I hated riding through the city traffic. We found ourselves on an on-ramp of an interstate, so had to do an about-face. State Police came along and stayed behind us on the next road so I thought we might get a traffic ticket, but didn't. We saw a school whose mascot name was the "Cornjerkers"!

DAY 36
Tuesday, July 23
Lafayette, IN to Portland, IN (105 miles)

Beautiful day for cycling – sunny but not too hot or humid, pleasant southwest breeze, gently rolling but predominantly level terrain. Passed through Hemlock, Indiana, where a tornado occurred four days ago. Trees and poles torn up, but no one was hurt. We stopped in some shade in the next town and an elderly man came out to chat. He got us a Coke and offered us the use of his bathroom. Such Midwestern generosity and hospitality. We ate lunch in Fairmont, Indiana, the home of James Dean. The restaurant was full of Dean's pictures and news clippings. Surprisingly, Dave didn't want to stop at the James Dean Museum! Ha ha!

It is amazing how many homes here in the Midwest fly the American Flag daily. We've seen so many hawks at close range that it's become commonplace. We enjoy seeing the little birds harass and even ride along on a hawk.

Found out (front page of local paper) that the "Wandering Wheels" tour came through town yesterday.

DAY 37
Wednesday, July 24
Portland, IN to Bellefontaine, OH (73 miles)

Terrain and weather very similar to yesterday, with some rain in the morning. Bellefontaine is the "Top of Ohio" at 1,549 feet. More hospitality from the locals: stopped to ask an older gentleman for directions and also got our bottles filled with water and ice cubes, and enjoyed the grandson's excited description of his visit to a theme park. We declined his offer to go around back and see the dogs. We are now back in the Eastern time zone.

Met an eighty-year-old man after lunch riding a Nordic Track bike. It has a belt brake and what he calls "automatic shift" with nine speeds. He claims to ride ten miles per day and 3,000 miles a year. When he is teased about riding to chores around town he jokes he is "waiting to get his snow tires off the car." We stayed at Mountain Top Inn, named tongue in cheek, I suppose.

DAY 42
Monday, July 29
LaVale, MD to Hancock, MD (46 miles)

Thanks to a lift from our son, Pete, we stayed overnight at our home in nearby Keyser. We didn't get back on the road in LaVale till mid afternoon the next day. Earlier, I went to Wal-Mart to get a plastic cover to make a second sign ("Seattle to NJ") and saw a friend from home, Bill C., and we talked for quite a while. Then we spent some time at Allegany Bike Works talking to Ed Taylor and crew. Ed kept telling us how proud of us he is; he is so excited about us doing this trip. Then we ate lunch at Wendy's where we ate with Allen S., and I was feeling nervous about crossing all the mountains before dark. But I didn't realize that Hancock was so close to Cumberland; we were there by 7:30 p.m.

I had a lot of stomach cramps from eating and then immediately riding. The mountains weren't actually too bad, I just didn't feel very well, and didn't go to dinner with Dave. Central Maryland is so pretty, but it was too overcast to appreciate. We had a flat tire today, a pinch flat caused by hitting a rock in the road.

DAY 43
Tuesday, July 30
Hancock, MD to Thurmont, MD (51 miles)   3,443 Total Miles to Date

Another day of ups and downs. It was mostly overcast again and we got to our motel thirty minutes before a tremendous downpour. We rode several miles on the C & O Canal towpath– just enough to get muddy. We saw a kingfisher. Memories of all the trips we've done on the canal and those friends with whom we rode: Andy, Skip C., Charlie W., Darrel and Mary Lou, Amy and Rob, Bud and Wes C. East winds today. It's taken forty-three days, but I found the perfect restaurant, Heavenly Gates, in Hagerstown, a Christian-run health food restaurant. I had a cold lentil tarragon salad, pasta primavera (even included squash), raisin muffin, and fruit cup. I wanted the apricot-mango cake roll with strawberries for dessert but it wasn't available so I had a "Hummingbird Angelette Cake" (small spice cake with pecans, pineapple, and coconut with a flower in the center). The waitress was very friendly; she plans to compete in the Olympics in the equestrian events. (She warned us not to stay in Thurmont because the Grand Dragon of the KKK lives there; I'm not sure where he was hiding but it was a pleasant enough town.)

The ride through the Catoctin Mountains was great, but as always, we didn't stop to see the falls, just flew on by. Stayed at the Cozy Inn, which has been visited by Winston Churchill, FDR, and many others, due to being so close to Camp David.

Dave's report: bottom bracket is clicking.

DAY 46
Friday, August 2
Monkton, MD to Odessa, DE (96 miles)

Hotter today and more hilly than we expected. Had planned to go to Dover but it was too far. We rode several miles on North Central Railroad (NCR) Trail trail before taking to poorly marked back roads. Spent half the day wondering where we were.

Crossed the Conowingo Dam over the Susquehanna River – pretty river above the dam and very shallow and rocky below it. Many waterfowl roosting on the rocks.

The click is louder in the bottom bracket. I asked Dave if I should sing in order to mask the noise (since it upset him). He didn't appreciate my humor.

Horrible city traffic in Newark, Delaware. I couldn't handle that on a single bike. Problems with my seat again, rocking back and forth. While talking at dinner, we both agreed that it's time for the trip to end. The biking has become boring, maybe partly because we're in our home territory, which we've biked before. Also, there's no more question of whether or not we'll make it or of what will happen next, so it's no longer a mental challenge. Also, the stops to visit with friends and family "broke the spell" as Dave so aptly put it. It was wonderful to see family, but it did make the trip feel completed before it actually was.

For whatever mistaken reason, we thought the two days from Towson (just outside Baltimore) to Ocean City, New Jersey, were going to be short and easy. Today was anything but! It wasn't particularly difficult but it wasn't easy. But we agreed that this is the appropriate way to finish the trip . . . worn out and tired.

DAY 47
Saturday, August 3
FINAL DAY
Odessa, DE to Ocean City, NJ (122 miles)

A day of surprises; headwinds almost constantly; much longer mileage than expected, bicycle maps very difficult to follow because many roads in Delaware aren't identified or labeled. We had to ride on major highways with the ocean traffic. (Thank goodness it was overcast.) We followed a scenic road to Bower's Beach right on the coast, had lunch and planned to take another scenic road down the coast. The waitress overheard our plans and hurried out to inform us that we couldn't get from Bowers Beach to South Bower's Beach on the road we wanted because there was no bridge across the river. There was only one way in and out of Bower's Beach, so we had to turn around and retrace our route.

We took the Cape May-Lewes ferry; it was a much longer ride than we had expected. Talked to awaiting family by cell phone. We had told them to expect us around 4:00 P.M. and it was after 6:00 when we got off the ferry. Mother had a TV crew and a news reporter there; I felt bad that the plans didn't work out. Dave and I sprinted the last thirty-six miles to Ocean City; my hamstrings protested!

Our reception at the ocean boardwalk was better than I could have imagined: The entire family was there with cameras and video cameras and the reporter had returned. We caused quite a commotion at the boardwalk entrance. The family serenaded us with "Daisy." Dave and I took the bike right into the surf and we got lots of pictures.

What a day, what a tremendous trip! Best experience of my life, besides being married to Dave!

47 Day Total: 3,710 miles

Appendix

Rhona and I rode a modified GT Quatrefoil tandem. It was originally equipped with 700 D hybrid wheels, but had been modified to use 700 C wheels by Allegany Bike Works (ABW). A Magura hydraulic brake was installed on the back wheel along with a drum brake. The front wheel was built by ABW. The rear wheel used Phil Wood hubs and was built by Totally Tandems in Iowa. The bottom brackets were Phil Wood.

It appears that worn timing gears, not the bottom brackets, caused the clicking sounds we heard late in the trip.

We started the trip with 28mm Kevlar GTK tires from Performance. Two of the three tires failed prematurely (one after only 300 miles). We purchased three Specialized Armadillo tires in Minot, North Dakota. The rear one lasted until Pittsburgh, Pennsylvania. The front tire appears to still have a lot of wear left in it.

We erred in not starting the trip with a new front and rear derailleur and replaced both of them during the trip. The Grip Shifters worked well. We both used bar ends on the handlebars and had to put additional padding on them to prevent pain. We used clipless pedals from Performance.

We started the trip with front low ride panniers, a sleeping bag on a front rack, a captain's handlebar bag, a stoker's handlebar bag, two rear panniers, a tent and two air mattresses on the rear rack. The setup was acceptable except in strong crosswinds. I'm not sure if pulling a single-wheeled trailer would have been a better idea while fully loaded. Just before we reached Glacier Park we sent twenty-six pounds of camping gear and clothing home. For the remainder of the trip we only had the handlebar bags, the rear panniers and a gym bag on the rear rack.

Dave lost approximately twenty-five pounds. Two weeks after finishing the trip, the captain had regained feeling in all but one toe (at one point six toes were partially numb). A sensation like an electrical charge is still felt when I grip something tightly. If I were planning to make the trip again on this tandem, I would add a flex stem of some kind to absorb the shock caused by the frost heaves on the western roads.

⛷ ⛷ ⛷

The unabridged version of this journal appeared as a series in the online newsletter of TOYS: Tandems of York (PA) Society.

BICYCLE TOURING IN YOUR OWN BACKYARD

By Theresa Russell

A prime cycling vacation is easy to come by and easy on the pocketbook,
that is, with a little help from your friends.

It certainly doesn't sound as glamorous as cycling in New Zealand or France, but your local area offers a wealth of opportunity easily overlooked. One major advantage of embarking on a tour from your own home is precisely that – you leave from home. No expensive airfares, no worries about getting to the station or airport, no surprise delays, no boxing your bicycle and no exorbitant charges to transport your bike. What could be better?

But what could possibly be interesting near your home? Well, that depends on your interests. Most counties have convention-and-visitors bureaus that will gladly send information about the area attractions, as well as a list of accommodations, campgrounds and restaurants. What appeals to you is a personal decision, but let

your imagination run wild. Perhaps a relative is buried in a certain cemetery and a visit there would aid your genealogical research. One poster on an e-mail list is organizing his route around attending minor league baseball games in his area. Perhaps a nearby town has a restaurant renowned for its ribs. Museums, festivals, architecture, historical sites, a bed and breakfast, county fair – whatever your interest, you are certain to find something.

Your trip may be short, perhaps just an overnight. But an overnight can be refreshing and rejuvenating. For a stay at a bed and breakfast, you could likely carry everything you need in a rack trunk. For a longer trip or a camping trip, you would obviously have to carry more supplies, and you would need additional equipment.

The Warm Showers List (www.warmshowers.org), a site maintained by Roger Gravel, is comprised of a group of cyclists who offer a place to sleep to other touring cyclists. This is a reciprocal list, meaning that all members agree to provide a minimum of a sleeping space, whether it is a tent site, floor space or a bed to other cyclists. This, in itself, could be a reason to choose a certain destination for your backyard tour. For more information visit this site and consider adding your name to the list.

Now, that you have a few options, you just need some free time and you can pedal right from your driveway to an exciting – personally interesting – destination.

᚛ ᚛ ᚛

CONTRIBUTORS

The writers and cartoonists who made this book possible.

Gianna Bellofatto (Reid) is a freelance writer, columnist, playwright and public relations professional. Life is a Bike© appears on *The Bicycle Exchange* and was nominated for the Pulitzer Prize in 2001. Other writing credits include off-off-Broadway plays, short stories, articles in *The Italian Tribune, Hudson Valley Life* and *The Nyack Villager*. "About Something©," her new column, appears in several newspapers throughout the U.S. Gianna is a graduate of the great late Upsala College. She resides in Pearl River, New York, with her husband, Steve Reid, who is a sculptor. She is an avid cyclist, enjoys photography, and wants to keep riding and writing. Reach her at jbwrites01@yahoo.com or visit www.lifeisabike.com.

James Brink is an attorney in private practice who lives, works, and bikes in and around Pittsburgh, Pennsylvania. He's been cycling for over twenty-five years. He is a member of the Western Pennsylvania Wheelmen and formerly of the Wheeling Area Bicycling Club. Jim's son, Eric, is a budding cyclist. Jim pedals a Trek 2120, a 1982 Trek 620, and a Trek 820 mountain bike. E-mail him at james.brink@att.net.

Born in Detroit in 1952, **Cathy Dion** got a new 20-inch Schwinn girls' bike for her sixth birthday. "I got on that bicycle and never looked back." Having ridden the Northern Tier across the U.S. in 1988, she says her "favorite" cycling is self-contained touring, though any time spent on her bike is her favorite riding. She usually commutes the forty-one-mile round trip to and from work and her stable houses a Rivendell Atlantis, a Bianchi Road bike and a mountain bike. She lives in Lake County, California, where she is always discovering new roads to ride and cycling experiences to write about in the journal she has kept up for forty-one years. Her work frequently appears in *Mason's Wire Donkey Bike Zine*. Her other interests include kayaking, gardening and bird watching. She lives with her companion of twenty-four years, four cats and one chicken in a small, old house with views of Clear Lake and Mount Konocti. "Oh, the sunsets!"

John Stuart Clark lives in Nottingham, England. Best known in Europe as *Brick* for cycling and political cartoons, he has traveled to every continent on the planet except Antarctica. His travel articles have appeared in every major UK cycling magazine and in many elsewhere in the world. He has also written on historical and social aspects of biking, and was the journalist who alerted consumers to the insecurity of D-locks back in the 1980s. He's had five books published, two about his travels and three of his cartoons. Contact him through www.brickbats.co.uk.

Alan Ira Fleischmann has been a serious cyclist since 1989, averaging 1,500 miles each year. A diabetic, freelance writer, and smoke shop owner, he has published books and articles on finance, science fiction, humor, cigars, education, and, of course, cycling. He rides a Trek OCLV 5200 road bike and a Fuji mountain bike. He has lived in Connecticut, New York, and Boston, but, since 1994, resides in Scott Depot, West Virginia, which he describes as "You're either goin' uphill, or you've got a killer headwind!"

Rhona and Dave Fritsch are originally from Peters Township in Southwestern Pennsylvania, but have lived in Keyser, West Virginia, since 1975. They are the parents of two grown children, daughter Kelly (and grandson Nicholas) in Towson, Maryland, and Peter in Waynesburg, Pennsylvania. Rhona is a reading teacher and Dave is a school transportation director. They have been bicycle touring together since 1989, frequently in statewide group tours. Other "big tours" have included a weeklong tour in the Colorado Rockies, the Canadian Rockies, the Cabot Trail in Nova Scotia, Ireland and the Netherlands. They purchased their first tandem in 1992 and their second after their cross-country tour. They have done portions of the Adventure Cycling Continental Divide route and hope to finish the route after retirement.

Jonny Hawkins is a full-time, professional cartoonist whose home is Sherwood, Michigan. His cartoons have appeared in over 300 publications, including widely read magazines like *Reader's Digest*, *Guideposts*, *Boy's Life*, *Harvard Business Review*, *Forbes*, and *Barron's*. He can be reached at jonnyhawkins2nz@yahoo.com.

Chip Haynes is a graphic artist and everyday cyclist living in Clearwater, Florida with his wife (The Lovely JoAnn) and about twenty bicycles. Chip enjoys folding bikes, fixed gear bikes, and, well, just about every sort of bike, if only he had the time to ride them all. His advice to cyclists: Keep your bike tires pumped. His advice to non-cyclists: When the oil runs out, they're all bike lanes. He can be reached at ehaynes@co.pinellas.fl.us.

Jill Homer is a newspaper editor living in Juneau, Alaska. When she isn't working, she likes to spend her time backpacking, hiking, canoeing and, most of all, bicycling. She recently completed a 3,200-mile, self-supported cycle tour from her front door in Salt Lake to Syracuse, New York. Visit her blog at arcticglass.blogspot.com.

Geoff Husband, ex-teacher, finally escaped Britain with Kate – long suffering touring partner and wife – to Brittany, France, in 1989, with a wild scheme to run lightweight cycletouring holidays. Breton Bikes (www.bretonbikes.com) managed to find enough customers mad enough to take it on and still thrives today. In his copious leisure time he has begun to expand into journalism and has been published in cycling magazines on three continents. Recent insane ideas include a charity ride in the Pyrenees (www.cycling-in-france.com) and pannier designs no one wants to make. He rides two Bob Jackson touring bikes, one green and heavy, one blue and whippy, and has played a small part in the production of three children, who he now tours with at every opportunity. He spends an average of ten weeks a year cyclecamping all over France and much of the rest of the year helping others do the same. Claim to fame? Managed to lose one and a half stone in ten days whilst leading a tour in the Auvergne with a stomach bug and still managed the last col (on his knees).

Thomas Hylton, a Pulitzer Prize-winning journalist, is author of a color coffee table book called *Save Our Land, Save Our Towns*. The book is a plea for comprehensive planning to save our cities, towns, and countryside. He is also host of an hour-long public television documentary called *Save Our Land, Save Our Towns*. The program has been broadcast prime time on all Pennsylvania PBS stations and has aired on more than 100 PBS stations nationwide. As president of Save Our Land, Save Our Towns Inc., a non-profit corporation, Hylton is an advocate of traditional towns that house people of all ages, races, and incomes. Since publication of the book, Hylton has given more than 300 presentations in Pennsylvania and thirty other states on land use planning and community building. He has addressed the National Governors' Association and has given talks to the legislators of both major parties in Pennsylvania. A native of Wyomissing, Pennsylvania, and a lifelong Keystone State resident, Hylton lives in Pottstown with his wife, Frances, an elementary school teacher. For twenty-two years, he wrote for Pottstown's daily newspaper, *The Mercury*. His editorials advocating the preservation of farmland and open space in southeastern Pennsylvania won a Pulitzer Prize in 1990. He remains an active leader in local planning commissions and preservation groups and his efforts have been recognized with awards from Preservation Pennsylvania, Pennsylvania Wildlife Federation, and Pennsylvania Forestry Association. Visit his organization's website at www.saveourlandsaveourtowns.org.

Bill Joyce has been known to do back-to-back English centuries from time to time. In addition to his cycling exploits, Bill's a darn good writer. His articles have appeared in numerous publications, including *The Daily Californian* and *The Catholic Voice*. A frequent traveler to Latin America, Bill's articles about the effects of civil war on children in El Salvador won him a national Catholic Press Association Award. When not cycling or writing, this citizen of Oakland, California, is doing what he does best of all – teaching. Oh, and he happens to be the oldest brother to the editor of this book. (*With age comes wisdom, or is it age before beauty, eh bro?* –The Editor). He can be reached at webike@yahoo.com.

Jim Joyce is the editor of this book, as well as the founder and editor of the online magazine, *The Bicycle Exchange*, a.k.a. Bikexchange.com. His articles (and photographs periodically) have appeared in the *Pittsburgh Post-Gazette*, *Bike Midwest*, the *Centre Daily Times* (State College, Pennsylvania), Penn State's *Daily Collegian*, the *Irish Edition*, and *All About Beer* magazine. A Western Pennsylvania native, he relocated to the Pittsburgh area in 1997, after a ten-year teaching career in Wheeling, West Virginia. He continues his teaching and, while he is very proud of *The Bicycle Exchange* and this book, he is most proud of being a teacher of adults and children who are blind. He resides in Emsworth, with lovely wife, Paulette, an award-winning registered nurse. He can be reached at ibike@bikexchange.com.

Ted Katauskas, Editor-In-Chief at *Portland Monthly Magazine*, bicycles to and from work every day on a hybrid he's ridden around the world. Before he moved to Portland, Oregon he commuted by Bridgestone from a Brooklyn Heights brownstone to a corner office at *The New Yorker*.

Bob LaDrew, who retired his photo processing business just before the digital camera boom, lives in rural Chester County, Pennsylvania, with his wife Judy. Together they produce the Delaware Valley Bicycle Club newsletter in which Bob's cartoon "Bonkerz" appears. The Bonkerz character has taken on mythical proportions within the club, just missing many rides. Bob, however, doesn't miss many, logging over 9,000 miles a year, during which many of the ideas for his strips germinate. He can be reached at 2ladrews@netreach.net.

Bob Lafay is a self-taught cartoonist who has viewed the sport of bicycling through a cartoonist's eye since 1991. Born and raised in Pennsylvania, he now resides in Tujunga, California. His cartooning career began when he was just twelve years old. His writing skills were so bad that his English teacher let him pass the class by illustrating his book reports instead of writing them. He thanks her dearly. Bob piloted hang gliders for over twenty-three years and published a book of cartoons on that subject. He has created well over 100 bicycling cartoons. After twenty-six years of engineering at Lockheed (commuting the last fifteen years) he took an early retirement. His travel adventures include riding from California to Pennsylvania on a road bike (later on a Harley) as well as excursions to Canada, Europe, China, Cuba and Guatemala. In January 2005 he finished his goal of mountain biking in all fifty U.S. states. Bob's cartoons have been published in *Hang Gliding*, *Wire Donkey Bike Zine*, *Dirt Rag* and various newsletters. To date, he's never missed a deadline.

He claims the biggest benefit of mountain biking is that he met the love of his life, Margie, on a bike. He can be reached at labikeboy@aol.com.

Ella Lawrence is a freelance writer from San Francisco, California. When not holed up in a café squinting intently at a laptop or a magazine, she can be found tutoring kids at 826 Valencia, getting muddy while racing cyclocross, or traveling throughout the world. She received her degree in Cultural Anthropology from the University of California and speaks five languages. She can say, "I'm going to drop you like a bad habit" in all of them. Find out more about her enormous appetites at www.ellalawrence.com.

Jay T. McCamic is a lawyer by trade and he and his wife, Jimmie Ann, enjoy tandem rides on their Burley Rock-N-Roll. They reside in Wheeling, West Virginia.

Scott Roberts has been a sports reporter on radio and in print since 1977. He has worked for various radio stations in Northwest Pennsylvania and has written for the Tri-City Edition of the *Erie Times-News*. Scott covered Pittsburgh Steelers home games as well as Super Bowl XXX. He also covered the Pittsburgh Pirates and, in 1981, covered the Major League All-Star Game and the NBA All-Star Game, both in Cleveland. He has done play-by-play and color commentary for high school football and has coached the sport at the seventh through twelfth grade levels. He has been an avid cyclist his entire life. His dream interviews would be Lance Armstrong and Greg Lemond.

Theresa Russell lived with her husband and children in the flatlands of northwestern Ohio before moving to Upstate New York. She began cycle touring in 1986, planning a month-long trip to New Zealand for an experiential learning program at the school where her husband, Robert, taught. She's returned to New Zealand three additional times for the same program and has also organized similar trips to Baja and the Yucatan. She and her husband authored the Midwest Edition (Ohio, Michigan and Indiana) of the Anacus Press *Bed, Breakfast & Bike* series (available at www.anacus.com). In addition she contributes to several national magazines. She is working on a guide to cycling in the Yucatan (Mexico), and on a travel site geared toward baby boomers – www.primetimetraveler.com.

Neal Skorpen spends most of his time in the basement, seeking The Perfect Brushstroke. His cartoons appear in humorous papers, alternative journals, and cycling magazines across the country. He also teaches computer graphics at The Art Institute of Portland. He has finally purchased real biking clothes, although he still wears the silly skull helmet. Visit his website at www.nealskorpen.com.

Andy Singer is a four-armed, six-legged alien from the planet Neptor. His multiple arms enable him to be a prolific cartoonist, while his huge jaws enable him to capture, crush and consume his favorite foodstuff – Sport Utility Vehicles. His cartoons have been compiled in a book, *No Exit*, which bears the same name as his comic strip. Andy's been published in many magazines and newspapers, and his work was once a daily feature in the *Saint Paul Pioneer Press*. Now he appears regularly in alternative newsweeklies like *Salt Lake City Weekly*, *Eugene Weekly*, *Athens News*, and *Random Lengths* in Burlington, Vermont. His cartoons have also appeared in the *Washington Post* and the *Boston Globe*, and the national magazines *Discover*, *The New Yorker*, *Esquire*, and *The Progressive*. Learn more about Andy at www.andysinger.com.

Mason St. Clair is eighty years old and has been a bike commuter ever since 1977. He has some two dozen bikes in his shed, builds his own wheels, and does his own mechanic work. He works part time as a water quality biologist with Nashville's (TN) Metro Water Services. He spent fifty years as a government biologist, (local, state, and federal USEPA). He "put the BURR in Bureaucrat." He's been cranking out the *Wire Donkey Bike Zine* ever since October of 1991, and has written some 1,000 limericks and clerihews. He can't stand recumbents, loves one-speeds, but also has and loves touring and racing bikes (he's got a Colnago Super that goes back to 1978). Says Mason: "Take care and keep those wheels a rollin.'" He can be reached at Masonbike@aol.com.

Freelance writer and editor, **Bradley Swink**, can be found, preferably waist-deep, in a Pennsylvania or Montana river fly-fishing for trout and steelhead. To pay the bills, he works as a creative and technical writer for a Fortune 500 company. The former competitive multi-sport athlete and bicycle racer resides in Springdale, Pennsylvania with his wife, Michele, and son, Holden. E-mail him at bradleyswink@yahoo.com.

Andy Wallen is president, salesman and technical consultant at Wheelcraft Bicycles in Wheeling, West Virginia. He and his wife, Cindy, operate the business and have two children. Andy has been in and out of the bicycle business since 1983. He has taught music in public and private schools, and has tutored homebound students. He is a part-time musician and wannabe mountain bike racer. He has logged tens of thousands of miles on his 1986 vintage Cannondale racing bike, and really likes his 1995 Gary Fisher Procaliber, Ltd. ("just like Paolo Pezzo's"). He is also the "Andy" of the *Bikexchange* "Ask the Mechanic" column. You can visit his shop's website at www.wheelcraft.us or e-mail him at ibike@bikexchange.com.

Nothing compares to the simple pleasure of a bike ride.
— John F. Kennedy

Thanks for giving this book a spin. Hope you enjoyed the ride!

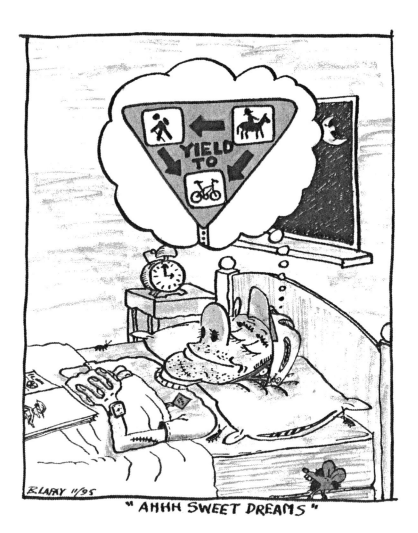

" AHHH SWEET DREAMS "